The Joy

of Travel

Have a great read!

Darlene Kidd

By

Darlene Ingram Kidd

Order this book online at www.trafford.com/07-1416
or email orders@trafford.com

Most Trafford titles are also available at major online book retailers.

Note for Librarians: A cataloguing record for this book is available from Library
and Archives Canada at www.collectionscanada.ca/amicus/index-e.html

Printed in Victoria, BC, Canada.

ISBN: 978-1-4251-3621-5

*We at Trafford believe that it is the responsibility of us all, as both individuals
and corporations, to make choices that are environmentally and socially sound.
You, in turn, are supporting this responsible conduct each time you purchase a
Trafford book, or make use of our publishing services. To find out how you are
helping, please visit www.trafford.com/responsiblepublishing.html*

*Our mission is to efficiently provide the world's finest, most comprehensive
book publishing service, enabling every author to experience success.
To find out how to publish your book, your way, and have it available
worldwide, visit us online at www.trafford.com/10510*

 www.trafford.com

North America & international
toll-free: 1 888 232 4444 (USA & Canada)
phone: 250 383 6864 ♦ fax: 250 383 6804 ♦ email: info@trafford.com

The United Kingdom & Europe
phone: +44 (0)1865 722 113 ♦ local rate: 0845 230 9601
facsimile: +44 (0)1865 722 868 ♦ email: info.uk@trafford.com

10 9 8 7 6 5 4 3

The Joy

of Travel

By

Darlene Ingram Kidd

Photo Legend:

Background, author samples the famous Guinness
  at the Guinness Brewery in Dublin, Ireland
Counterclockwise from upper left:
Husband, Pat, and author's cousin, Eliz Laurie,
  manoeuvre the canoe at Kingsmere River Landing
Author and friend, Heather Jellis, set off on their first
  hike in the Yorkshire Dales
Author poses in the stocks before the
  Old Courthouse in Aldborough, England
English walking friend, Joan Kirk, poses with an
  unexpected friend on the Yorkshire Moors
Back cover: Author at the Upper Lake at Glendalough,
  Wicklow Mountains, Southern Ireland

Dedicated to travel companions on the road of life

There is no frigate like a book
To take us lands away,
Nor any coursers like a page
Of prancing poetry.
-Emily Dickenson(1830-86)

Contents

Paths of the World

Paths of Home

Circling Paths

PATHS OF THE WORLD

THE PEE AND THE HANDBRAKE

Erica had saved like a hound squirreling away bones for winter. She had worked for the previous two summers and had even earned enough to pay for her own tuition at University each fall. Now nearing the end of her second year, which would qualify her as a teacher with a Standard A certificate, Erica knew that all her saving was going to work out. Her very first student loan had sufficed and she had stretched it with very careful planning plus many care packages from home. She toyed with the idea of suggesting to her mother that the two of them take that long-awaited trip to Scotland.

Mom was a war bride and had never been home. Erica knew that her mother had yearned for nothing more for the past twenty-one years. So during the Christmas holidays they considered the idea and decided to at least get their passports. During the February break they visited a travel agent and bought the tickets — Winnipeg to Prestwick return. Prestwick was still 100 miles from the Borders but they would rent a car — Erica would drive.

In March Erica signed a contract for a teaching position for the next year. She was offered her old summer job back again — Erica accepted notifying her employers that she would need three weeks off in early June. Details were falling into place.

On May 28, 1968, Erica and Mom boarded the bus to take them

1

to Winnipeg.   Later that day they boarded a Ward Air jet to
Prestwick.   Neither had flown before and the thrill and attention
they received on board was phenomenal.   Meals every two hours.
Airline stewardesses in lovely blue, pleated suits, hovering over
them at all times.   Such service had hitherto been unknown in
Erica's short life and as for Mom—she was usually the one doing all
the serving.
    They arrived in Prestwick in brilliant 8 am spring sunshine.   The
car rental agent had some tense moments when he discovered that
Erica was only 19—he insisted that the rental agreement was only
good for 21-year-olds.   Mom stuck to her guns—she would not
drive.   Erica was willing and at 19 nothing could dampen the spirit.
She could handle the situation and the car.   The agent agreed to take
her for a short test drive to ascertain her driving skill.   Erica passed
with flying colors.   They were on their way.   Only 100 miles to go—
no problem, they could be there in a couple of hours.
    A few wrong turns in Kilmarnock slowed their progress but
once they tried an alternate route they found the correct highway
and out into the country they went.   Not quite sped, the two had
miscued as to the condition, width, variety of dips, and curves on
the asphalt roads.   Indeed, they had only 100 miles to go but as the
morning proceeded they became very aware that they would not
cover 100 miles in two hours as they did back in Saskatchewan.
However, the scenery was magnificent.   They were in rare form and
sunshine accompanied them along the way.
    Thankful that the route did not lead through many towns as
that simplified driving, Erica and Mom eventually became aware
that they would need to visit the bathroom.   Both needed to pee
desperately.   They watched carefully and soon found a quiet field
where they could pull off the road and squat behind the wall.   From
the small knoll they overlooked a vista of pure, pastoral beauty—
green hills rolling away in the distance under a canopy of glistening
sunshine.
    Mission accomplished, they both felt very much refreshed and
ready to be on their way.   Erica had set the handbrake before
disembarking from her car as the terrain was rolling and uneven.
Now she was faced with removing the brake.   Try as she might it
would not release.   Erica encountered the first doubts of her driving
experience!   For a tense quarter of an hour she and Mom tugged at

the stubborn stick between them—pushing and twisting and yanking. It would not budge! They were beginning to get warm now, aided by the sunshine and the anxiety of the situation.

Just as they were certain that they would spend the remainder of their lives sitting in the lovely Scottish sunshine until they died of starvation, two Scottish gallants whirled by in their car. Erica and Mom sheepishly signalled their distress.

Two good-natured youths alit laughing their amusement at the stranded Canadian women's plight. Their laughter only increased at Mom's explicit description of the situation. Diplomatic she was not. To lie about the situation or even spare the details had never crossed her mind! The tale only served to increase their enjoyment.

They laughed and talked a mile a minute in their broad, Scottish tongues as they glibly and easily eased up on the handbrake pushing in on the end button at the same time. So easy, when you knew how! Embarrassed but thankful the women made their apologies and breathed overindulgent thanks, as Erica ground into reverse and accelerated down the highway.

The last view in her rear-view mirror was of two mightily-entertained Scottish lads standing on the highway smiling broadly and bewilderedly from ear to ear.

THE OTHER SIDE OF THE CURTAIN

Erica rolled on her side, her nightgown wrapped about her waist and thighs. It was still early in terms of another sleepless night. 2 am—she had already been to the bathroom twice and helped herself to a glass of water from the fridge in their Mexican hotel room. Even though she had the bathroom light on, Ripley slept on. He hadn't even turned over on the other side of the king-sized bed.

Erica hesitated before getting up again. The hard mattress that ordinarily felt delicious after a long day of swimming, hiking, and working out was impossible. There was just nowhere in the bed that offered comfort. She slid to her feet and wandered again to the bathroom, again to the fridge, and back to the bedside again. Searching the darkened room for an avenue of distraction, Erica considered that perhaps a few minutes on the third-floor deck might offer some entertainment and eventually induce relaxation, the precursor of sleep.

Glancing again at the bed and satisfied that Ripley was deeply asleep she carefully parted the heavy insulating curtains and then the sheers. Closing them tightly behind her to keep in the cool air from the air conditioner, she quietly unlocked the patio door and slid the screen open enough for her to step out onto the cement patio.

Fog enveloped the surrounding acres. Street lights shone

4

casting a ghost-like haze. Crickets chirped. The disco was silent or at least the dance music was not reaching her ears. The night was peaceful. Why then was she unable to sleep? Maybe now I will drop off she thought.

She turned her back on the outdoors. Erica reached for the screen and the patio door. Stepping inside she turned to close the screen and then the patio door. Once it was closed she fumbled to lock the patio door in the dark.

Wham! Suddenly the curtain struck her. Briefly she wondered if this might be Ripley's idea of a prank and had thrown a shoe at the curtain to scare her.

Before she could move, the curtain was being battered—wham, wham—the blows striking her again and again.

Was this some huge, crazed bat that had been trapped in their room trying to escape?

Terrified, she gave a loud and piercing scream, "Ripley, Ripley, help!"

"Someone's trying to break into our room," he shouted and flailed another resounding thud that glanced off her arm and struck her breast.

Raising her arms in defence, "It's me! It's me!"

The curtain hung limp; pulling it aside, she peered into the darkened room. There stood Ripley, naked back towards her, staring at the empty bed.

Turning, "WHAT were you doing OUT THERE? Oh, my God! Where did I hit you?"

Speechless, she pointed to her arm and breast.

For the first time in thirty years of marriage, Erica heard him breathe, "I'm sorry" as he rubbed her arm.

Clinging to Ripley in disbelief, relief, and exhaustion, "You've got to stop watching those scary movies before you kill someone."

Hysterical giggles bubbled up, "My screams—do you think the people next door heard me—what will we tell Security if they come?"

Weak from fright, the couple attempted to go back to bed. But the shock of the fright they had given each other only produced more uncontrollable, nervous giggles. Erica opened her bedside book. She felt her arm—Oh, no. She was bleeding. Ripley expressed disbelief but for the second time tonight began to realise that this night could produce any surprise.

As Ripley searched in his wallet for a bandaid for her arm, Erica checked the sheets for blood. How would they explain the screams AND THEN THE BLOOD ON THE SHEETS? As she wiped blood from the lower sheet, discovered and sponged some from the pillow case, and then even the upper sheet, Ripley reacted with shocked disbelief to the drops of blood he discovered on the floor. He hurried to wipe them up with bathroom tissue.

Giggles were still emanating from their throats as they nervously awaited the Mexican security personnel from the hotel—the language barrier, the scream, the blood—how would they ever convince anyone that the events in their room were innocent. What must the people in the adjoining rooms be thinking?

Erica read her novel. She shook her head as Ripley tuned into yet another scary movie. Finally after two hours of giggling and no evidence of security personnel, Erica and Ripley settled down to sleep.

In the morning, Erica took the paper down to Gloria and Peter, friends they had made at the resort. She queried, "Do you see anything different about me?"

Peter was quick to comment on her bandaid. The story produced hilarious laughter followed by the sober realisation of what might have happened. How does a husband explain his wife mysteriously falling from a third-story deck at 2 o'clock in the morning?

The next week, home from the trip, Erica remembered her doctor's appointment for a medical. She prayed for the bruises to fade but no such luck. With her courage packed tightly she set off in minus 37 degree Celsius weather for the neighbouring town and her check up. She sat for what seemed like hours awaiting her 9 am appointment. No one seemed to be invited into the inner sanctum although there were two other people in the waiting room. She waited in faked cheerful anticipation. What if the doctor were to be suspicious of her bruises? He had to be—that was his job. Still Erica prattled on with another lady in the waiting room about the temperature, the folly of holidaying in Mexico last week when the weather at home was fine and returning to the shock of this.

Finally the attendant asked, "Erica, did you have an appointment?"

"Yes."

"What time and with whom?"   By now it was 9:20 am.

"Dr. Twimdel at 9 am."   She answered.   "I made the appointment at least a month ago."

"Dr. Twimdel is in surgery and will be there until 10:30. Sorry."

With that she approached another young lady in the waiting room. As Erica left the room she passed the second lady.

"Who were you to see?" she ventured.

"Dr. Trimdel."

"What time?"

"9 am."

The situation was inconvenient to be sure. However as Erica climbed back into the freezing car which creaked its resistance as she eased it out of the parking lot, she couldn't help but consider herself and Ripley fortunate. At the very least they had escaped the embarrassment of an investigation. One more example of the excellent care the good Lord takes of his poor, dear ignorant children. When the appointment was rescheduled a month later, the bruises were only a distant memory.

DISNEY WORLD—HERE WE COME

Maria and Susan had planned and waited for this first independent trip. Maria had travelled a lot but always with her parents. Susan had never travelled.

They left their hometown of Sharit just as the tip of orange, April sun was peaking above the horizon. Although Maria was fortressed in the back seat with her pillow and a blanket hoping to enjoy a little more sleep, their excitement was too much to be contained. They chattered away as Maria's mother drove and soon they had put distance between them and home. Sixty miles had fallen away before Maria pulled out her itinerary, double checking for tickets and the required documents. Yes, I have both sets of tickets. She read that airline passengers would need to have some picture ID. Instantly Susan's expression grew dark and troubled. She blurted, "Oh, no! Lynden told me to get rid of all the extra stuff in my purse and I didn't bring my driver's license. I have no picture ID."

Mother slowed to a halt. They had just passed a small town. Hopefully it had a pay phone where they might call for someone at Susan's home to meet them with the driver's license. Cruising the town, it was obvious that it hadn't a pay phone. They had crossed the edge of a time zone in their short trip and the residents of Mattin were really not stirring much yet. Finally they noticed lights in one window. Susan, feeling very much a fool, timidly knocked on the door and used her calling card to call home. Her dad would meet them half way.

Retracing their trip for 30 miles was boring but necessary. Off they went and the driver's license was retrieved. Luckily it was Easter Holidays and Dad was not at work.

Optimism restored, the threesome again set off for Edmonton. Time flew as they were truly awake now. It became apparent that they must have a light lunch before doing the last leg to the airport. That accomplished, the group pressed on—their plentiful allotment of time had become just a comfortable amount of time to get the girls to the airport, two, rather than three hours, before takeoff.

Finally Mom dropped the girls at the departure bay and went to park the car. She hurried into the airport to say the last goodbyes. Mom, too, was on Easter Break and was looking forward to a leisurely evening with her friend in Edmonton and shopping the following morning before she returned home. However, approaching the check-in line-up, she encountered some fallen faces. The girls had advanced through the short line-up quickly and were standing to the side apparently waiting for something. Whatever could have gone wrong!

Now Susan was crying. The airport ticket supervisor was phoning the Customs Office—Susan hadn't brought her birth certificate. Mom could tell that, by now, relations between Maria and Susan had become somewhat strained. She sought to soothe and smooth the waters. The ticket supervisor had a reply now—she was sorry, the airline could allow the girls to leave Canada but Susan would not be granted re-entry without her birth certificate. Susan pled—could she get a copy faxed to her in Florida. The answer was negative—must have original. Travel today was impossible but the girls could fly tomorrow if they could get the birth certificate.

Again the disappointed group sought the telephone and Susan again called home. Dad would meet them again but not half way— he insisted that he drive to Camrose—2/3 of the total distance to the airport. Wait in the mall. He would come there.

A dejected group retraced their miles to Camrose and wandered the mall, long and beseechingly. The girls tried shopping but their hearts were not in it. They had another light lunch. Finally after waiting what seemed like hours, Susan spotted her dad walking briskly down the mall clutching her purse in his arms.

Smiles of relief greeted him amid questioning glances concerning the purse.

He explained, "I brought your entire purse in case you needed some other identification. And I've had to hitch-hike the last 30 miles. With your luck today, I didn't dare leave the purse in case the car was broken into." We stared in disbelief—had to hitch-hike?

"I ran out of gas!"

"I'll just go to Canadian Tire and buy a gas can. If you could just take me to the Petro-Can station I'll buy a little gas and get you to drive me back to the car."

Failing to believe the set of events through which they had lived this day, the group loaded up the gas can and headed back, hoping but not hopeful, that the car would really be where it was left. They joked, choosing to look on the bright side of the day's events and discussing what a wonderful story this would be to write one day.

Amazingly there she was. The miracle of the day! Not one hubcap missing. There she sat on an approach just slightly to the right of the road. Not stolen, not broken-into, and not even cold yet. Shiny, unscratched, locked and safe. They waited. Yes, she even went easily and this time the girls headed west and Dad headed east. Susan hugged her purse with all her documents tightly to her aching stomach.

So much for the leisurely evening and the morning shopping trip. Mom spent the evening in bed nursing a whopper of a headache while the girls went to a movie.

The next morning Mom drove the girls to the airport. Surprisingly, shopping no longer held the allure that it had when they first left. She left immediately for home.

THE BIRTH CERTIFICATE

Mary's voice was a drone of dismay. "Erica, I've left my birth certificate at home and I need it for our trip to Palm Springs."

Erica held the phone and thought this one should not be too bad to solve. But the plot meandered through deeper bog. Mary was on Vancouver Island with her daughter. Erica was Mary's next-door neighbour in Saskatchewan.

"I need you to get the key for my suite from the complex manager and (and here the plot got more twisted) get my safety deposit box key from the container on the desk in my study. On Monday I need you to go to the bank and go into my safety deposit box and get my birth certificate and mail it to me by priority post." All this was beginning to sound like espionage—at least like a major breach in a security system set up to protect people.

Erica listened with horror to the details of the mission she was agreeing to carry out. Who could have master-minded such an operation! Well, she would do what she could within the confines of the law to get this birth certificate to Vancouver Island before December 29. It was already December 20.

And, Mary continued, "Can you contact the complex manager and see if you can get her to agree to let you into my suite?"

Erica made the call quickly and was astounded at the swift co-operation from the manager. It all seemed a bit too easy except that rather than go out tonight and open the suite they would do it tomorrow. But tomorrow Erica had two church services to lead plus

11

a church Christmas supper to host as president of the United Church Women's organization. She had food to prepare for the men at home and food to take for the potluck supper. December 21 was their thirtieth wedding anniversary as well.

She quickly phoned back to Mary who had called the bank manager and he, too, seemed only too willing to see this fly. Erica blinked at the smoothness of the whole identity operation. ONLY IN SASKATCHEWAN!

10 am, the home church had been set up for the supper. The tables were set. The food dishes were prepared and waiting to be baked. Noon, one church service was complete. 2 pm, Erica was back in town. She quickly called the complex manager to indicate her readiness for operation #1.

"Can I pick you up now?" Erica enquired.

The reply was not nearly as co-operative as the previous evening.

"Well, I need Mary to phone me herself. Even though your name is listed as an emergency contact (surprise to Erica was this news) the board members don't think I should allow your admittance without prior authorization from Mary. Could you just have her call me?"

This sounded logical enough but time was beginning to run short in Erica's day. Calls to Vancouver Island from Saskatchewan at 2 pm were arriving at noon. The family was out to church followed by brunch. This necessitated a couple more hours delay. Erica just wanted to have this step of the operation behind her.

Shortly afterward a call came from Mary who had read the call display. "Complex manager wants a call from you."

"Right, will do immediately."

Knowing it was not likely that the manager would call Erica back, Mary called to assure Erica that the affair was a go.

The deed was done. Every step progressed exactly according to instructions.

Still Erica felt just a tad like a thief.

The evening Christmas festivities proceeded without a hitch.

Sharply at 9 am the following day Erica was at the bank clutching the safety deposit key, assured that she would be admitted to the safety deposit box. However, again there seemed to be just a shade of hesitation as the assistant manager produced a faxed letter from Mary(another surprise to Erica) and another release form for Erica to sign. Another bank attendant hovered close during the opening of the box and the extraction of the birth certificate. She signed both pieces of paper along with Erica signifying the validity of the whole operation.

Quickly Erica fled the premises. She stuffed the birth certificate in the prepared envelope and made for the post office. Finally the document was registered and dispatched by priority post with assurance that it would arrive in two days or less.

The next evening Erica was relieved to hear Mary's cheerful voice. "It's here. Merry Christmas!"

THE LURE OF YORKSHIRE

December 1979:
   This story begins with a near-fatal car accident. Erica suffered only bad bruises and cracked ribs even though the car fared much worse. While recuperating Erica searched her Saskatchewan home for reading material in the form of a lightweight book that she could hold aloft long enough to satisfy her unquenchable thirst for MORE. She found just that in her three-and-half-year-old farmer-boy son's bookcase, a trilogy of paperbacks given to him by a friend. They were written by James Herriot and Erica devoured them in 10-minute intervals—just long enough to finish a story before her arms and ribs became weak from elevating the book so that she could read it from her reclining position. As she replaced the book on the floor beside her, Erica was unfailingly overcome by quiet amusement coupled with feelings of the warmth and contentment penned by one who tramped the hills. Thus she healed.
Fall, early 1980s:
   Erica confided to her childhood friend, Simone, living in Edmonton, Alberta, that someday in her retirement she would walk the hills and dales where James Herriot worked.
   Turning to Erica, Simone replied, "Don't go without letting me know when you intend to do that. I would like to do it too."
   They nursed their dream silently and separately as they went to work, 200 miles apart, each day; coached their children through education, childhood aches, pains, joys, and university, and aged

14

two decades.
February 1996:

Erica was told she needed surgery. Not convinced but resigned she went to the hospital armed with an arsenal of James Herriot books—healing for the body and soul. She was back teaching school in just four weeks.

November 1997:

Erica and Simone were now discussing, "Can we wait for retirement? Should we? Maybe we should do it now?"

The ailments of younger friends and a sibling were causing them concern, "What if we were to be stricken ill before retirement?"

Their research intensified. Where was Darrowby, Yorkshire, anyhow? How small can it be that not one single map has it listed. Finally a Yorkshire native daughter living in Kelvington, Saskatchewan, Erica and Simone's hometown, suggested that they talk with her sister living in Kirkby Malzeard, Yorkshire. They resisted, not wanting to inconvenience anyone. Erica tried a travel agent. Not much luck. She wrote to the British Tourist Agency—information was overwhelming and not specific enough. Were the offered trips really what and where they wished to visit? Finally, in almost desperation, Erica contacted the Yorkshire Connection.

The response was instant and perfect. "I, too, have been wanting to do the Herriot Way. Please feel free to make our house your base until we start our walk."

July 1998:

And so they did. Erica and Simone trudged the 55 miles of the Herriot Way through rain, and wind, and the odd drop of lovely sunshine—but the scenery and the company and the hospitality! On the last day as they slogged their way through to the finish line, they dropped to a park bench in the square of Askrigg to have their picture taken before the famed Skelgill House of the television series based on James Herriot's books "All Creatures Great and Small".

When they returned to Canada and had written their 'Thank you' notes, Erica was sure that the Yorkshire Connection would end. She went back to her busy teaching schedule and their hosts would return to their active retirement and family obligations. But the letters kept coming, and even a phone call, until Erica found she needed the connection. She was internally driven to keep up the Yorkshire Connection. She was smitten—returning in summer 1999, and would have again in 2001 but for FMD (foot and mouth disease).

February 2002:

Erica's mother and sister arrived for a short visit. After feasting, visiting, and card playing Erica climbed the stairs for much-needed rest before work the next day.

Her mother tossed a sheaf of papers on her bed, "You'll enjoy this. You like history."

Erica gathered up the eleven-page family tree to give it a cursory glance before she relegated it to her bedside table for later reading.

At the first line, "David Middleton, b. Askrigg, Yorkshire, England" her drooping eyelids flew open and her heartbeat quickened. Erica was hooked—no sleep until the remainder of the document was read.

This was her family.

She had heard that her paternal great-grandparents, the Christopher (son of aforementioned David) Middleton family, had emigrated from England to Peterborough, Ontario, and Frobisher, Saskatchewan. However, both great-grandparents were dead years before Erica was born. Their daughter, Erica's grandmother, lived 300 miles from Erica's parents. And although Grandmother told of her parents coming from England, England seemed farther away than the moon from a small Saskatchewan farm in the 1950s. It was not a place Erica imagined or even read about anyone visiting. That's the reason she never asked the details of their homeland.

But in February 2002, Erica suddenly cared and cared very much. She couldn't wait to telephone her Yorkshire friends and tell them about her recent discovery.

"Let us go to St. Oswald's Church and look for the headstone. We'll check the church records. You may still have relatives there."

Just six days after Erica's initial discovery her Yorkshire friends were in Askrigg enquiring. And they were successful. Later at their home in Kirkby Malzeard they continued to rethink the startling coincidence of it all. A closer look at the book for the 'Herriot Way' disclosed that Erica had actually walked past the garden gate of the home from which her great-grandparents had emigrated.

Simone probably termed it just right when told of their news, "No wonder, you are so drawn to keep returning to Yorkshire. It's in your blood."

As a result of the Askrigg investigations, the researcher of the family tree wrote to relatives in Yorkshire. The replies came quickly via e-mail expressing interest and welcoming those North Americans so inclined to visit.

July 2002:

Erica made another wonderful trip to the hills and dales of Yorkshire revisiting many sites from the first trip and this time with another purpose—to visit the spots from which her ancestors emigrated and to meet many people descended from their shared great-great-grandfather.

If one thinks only of each piece of the puzzle independently, each seems a simple and innocent occurrence. However, taken together, the events seem to have had an almost mystic power. One wonders if all those occasions could have been purely accidental. So many quirks of nature and events to have transpired in just the right time, place, and order to achieve the marvellous discovery! Or was there an underlying purpose for each event to have happened in that particular sequence? What does matter is that Erica met more wonderful Yorkshire people and the greenery of the Yorkshire hills was a brilliant contrast to the stark plains of drought-stricken Saskatchewan in this summer of 2002. Some would say that Erica found her centre, her roots.

September 2003:

Barbara Batten (Middleton descendent) of Shrewsbury, England, alights at Saskatoon airport from Toronto. She has recently been visiting in Peterborough, Ontario, with other Middleton descendents. Barbara and Erica are off on a Canadian adventure across the prairies and through Alberta and British Columbia to meet as many Canadian Middleton descendents as they can squeeze into 15 days. What a wonderful, small and exciting world!

THE ROSE AND CROWN

Wensleydale
sunny Sunday afternoon
multiple generations
distant kin and in-laws
sharing common great-great-grandfather
reaching hands, hearts, and smiles
across countries, continents, and miles
exploring family mysteries from 1884

deep roots restored
over roast lamb and beef
and five nonagenarians

stellar fellowship
at the Rose and Crown

Bainbridge, Yorkshire
October 10, 2005

WORLD CLASS DINING

Sharon and Jacob loved the atmosphere of a good restaurant—the rush of the aroma of good food served with pizzazz, the surge of power watching others enjoying, chatting and generally making merry, the feeling of reckless abandon that comes when someone else prepares and serves. This was the height of class! It was the extravaganza of Lucy's in Las Vegas. Along with Tom and Linda, they were savouring the exotic offerings on the menu, the musical accompaniment and the unusual Californian décor.

As soon as their orders had been taken, the couples settled back for some decadent visiting and enjoyment of the surroundings. The establishment was teeming with unusual and interesting people dressed in a variety of entertaining styles. Obviously everyone in this town was wired for a good time. Drinks flowed. Food smelled of spicy blends. Spirits rode high.

The couples spoke of lofty dreams and plans for their lives—businesses that would never fail. The energy that they felt today would surely see them to the moon. Their pigs would fly!

Although in their forties, each of the foursome felt an energy that they had not experienced since their twenties. And this time they had the knowledge of forty-year-olds to direct that energy. What feelings of empowerment. Each was brimming over with imagination and plans. "What if we...what if a guy tried...maybe we...investment...."

Sharon vaguely noticed a bowl of liquid on a small plate had

been placed in front of her. Not skipping a beat in the excitement of
the conversation, she poised her soup spoon and carefully lifted a
spoonful of the steaming liquid to her lips. Slowly swallowing, she
wondered at the blandness of the soup but zeroed in on the
conversation and sipped on. The euphoria of the dining experience,
beautiful surroundings and enlightened minds carried the moment.
She ladled up the contents of the bowl and set it to the edge of the
table. The waiter, ever polite, whisked the empty bowl and its plate
quietly away.   Sharon wondered if she noticed a strange
questioning look in his expressionless eyes as he paused ever so
slightly in the fluid motion with which he scooped up the dishes.

When the entrees appeared, Sharon stared at her plate of
barbeque beef ribs in disbelief. A dignified upper lip carried the
day. She continued on with her meal knowing that her friends
would likely not perceive her faux pas in their heightened state.

The flavours, spices, aromas, and auras all contributed to a
savoury meal mingled with a feeling of heightened relaxation. The
group was mellowed out, relaxed, and jolly.

Jacob excused himself politely and found his way to the men's
room. The meal had been exquisite, but he would feel much more
comfortable after this visit.   Then he could resume his leisurely
conversation with his wife and friends and extend this pleasant
evening far into the night. The company was inspiring—when had
he felt so empowered in the presence of such congenial people.
Jacob took his time, relaxing and even noticing the tastefulness of
the bathroom décor.

Emerging from the men's room, Jacob was impressed and
somewhat overwhelmed by the number of smiling visages that
were turned in his direction as he returned to his table. These
people were fabulous. Such friendliness! Acknowledging their
smiles with his own smile and an almost imperceptible wave, Jacob
wove his carefree way back to his table. He quietly slid onto his
chair.

At the end of the lovely and lengthy evening of entertainment
and visiting, Jacob and Sharon arrived back at their condo. Jacob
removed his overcoat to discover a long length of bathroom tissue
suspended from his belt and draped down the back of his dress
pants. His face fell a mile! Sharon smothered a peal of laughter,
remembering that she, too, had contributed her moment of hilarity

and embarrassment to a flawless evening.   She had, after all, consumed the contents of her finger bowl.

HONEYMOONING IN MOSCOW(1974)

The Iron Curtain was still intact.

The Saskatchewan Teachers' Federation was offering an Easter flight to Moscow spending a few days in each of Moscow and St. Petersburg. In 1974 this might be the only route by which to gain access to a relatively inaccessible country.

Lois and Jeff decided to go. They had eloped, just three months earlier, to the church behind their house and become man and wife. What more interesting honeymoon could they hope for!

Remembering to pack their marriage license seemed the most unusual preparation that they could expect to make—Lois remembered that accommodation facilities in Italy, and other Roman Catholic countries, had sometimes required those documents of other young couples before allowing them to share a room.

Culture shock began at the Moscow airport with its distinctive aroma of urine. Buses were adequate, if interesting, in the manner in which they were driven. Gasoline was at a premium even then. So the driver had developed a unique habit of accelerating rapidly until he reached the speed limit or beyond, then throwing the transmission into neutral and coasting for as far as possible before throwing the gear box into gear and repeating the process all over again. Not a restful ride after being in the air some 36 hours during various legs of the journey.

Accommodation was in the luxurious, by Russian standards,

Intourist Hotel.

Upon opening the hotel room door another treat was in store for the newlyweds—single beds placed head to head. Well that problem could be overcome.

The week was spent in a frenzy of tours. Meals were again luxuriant by Russian standards, ample portions of mashed potatoes, topped off with plenty of red cabbage. Dessert was invariably ice cream with its own distinctive flavour—if served in a cone, the cone tasted of paper. And everything else was garnished liberally with green onions.

The only grocery stores they encountered were street-side barrows selling only three items—tea, lemons, and bread. Shopping for souvenirs was executed in a special store only for tourists— Russian citizens were not welcome there. Most items were cast iron—candle holders, strange stacking hedgehogs, shields with coats of arms on them, busts of Lenin, fur hats, and huge fur coats into which Lois could have easily fit at least four of her bodies.

Tours of museums, art galleries, the tomb of Lenin, and a Russian school where dance lessons, mathematics lessons and a drama performance of "The Mad Hatter's Tea Party" were in progress entertained the Canadian troop. They surveyed the exterior of churches and noted the elderly entering and leaving in a quiet, low key manner. Streets were cleaned by elderly women using twig brooms. And the military did everything else—maintain the streets, fix the roads, deliver the mail, shift our baggage at the airport into rough-hewn hayracks for transport.

The group of Canadians attended the opera and fell asleep. After witnessing the Russian citizens leaving their seats and travelling in hordes up a lengthy escalator at Intermission, they thought the performance was finished and exited for their hotel. Only later would they discover that the citizens who had been working long hours all day went to the cafeteria at intermission to finally have a meal.

Lois and another friend had their hair done in the beauty parlour of the hotel one morning. How interesting to watch the same beer that they drank at night dyed purple and used for setting lotion and hairspray! Meanwhile Jeff and friend's husband were involved in their own quest—they sought to take a taxi ride to a farm. First of all no taxi driver seemed to want to have them.

Finally a driver jumped in another man's cab and began to drive them from one side of the city to the other. Each time John showed the driver the Russian word for 'farm' which a hotel attendant had written, the cabbie took off in another direction. After much hurtling about the city at a breakneck pace, the men managed to see exactly nothing of Russian farm life.

Each floor of the hotel was square with rooms all around the edge. Upon leaving a hotel room, occupants were required to hand in the key to the desk womaned by two women who appeared to supervise the cleaning staff for that floor.

Finally one morning the honeymooners decided that this constant touring was becoming a bore. They would enjoy a morning to themselves and join the tour at lunch. Of course they had breakfast in the dining room with the rest of the group at 8 am sharp. Afterwards they returned to bed.

Lois had just rested her head. Jeff was in the washroom. The doorbell rang. They ignored it hoping the intruder would go away. The ringing sounded again more urgent this time. Again the couple ignored it and again the ringing sounded followed by long and insistent rapping. Lois threw the top sheet over her nude body and crept to the door. Opening it she surveyed the solidly-built deskwoman with a man carrying some gadget. Lois indicated that they were not interested in company and closed the door. Seconds later the doorbell sounded again. She opened the door to the same entourage. Again Lois indicated that they didn't want whatever was being offered and closed the door. Again the bell rang. Clutching her sheet around her, while Jeff scrambled into his pants, they again checked the door. This time the woman and man all but forced their way into the room.

Lois and Jeff could only stand in disbelief as the woman assumed a no-nonsense pose dead-centre in the middle of the room while the man engaged his gadget and began his search under the beds, over the nightstands and lights, into the bathroom, over the taps, and under the toilet. And then it was over!

Obviously they were clean, for though they waited for more knocks and rings, none came! The morning passed not quite as leisurely as they had planned but they definitely provided the lunch hour entertainment with their tales of the morning's espionage.

DIVINE INTERVENTION

Meredith pinched herself. The week had been sublime. It was a glorious break from the crops and cattle back home in Saskatchewan.

She and Terry along with their children, Sarah and Corey, and their niece, Sherri had shared a tremendous respite of sunshine at their favourite Easyfair Mountain Resort. They had lounged for hours by gorgeous waterfalls, visited the Columbia Icefields riding up on the huge IceMobile to lofty heights and actually walked on the glacier. They had picnicked, fished and wiener roasted. They had hiked to the White Rabbit Forest Reserve and reached the crest of the White Rabbit Falls. Meredith had actually had the opportunity to interview some outfitters who operated just across the road from the resort. So while Terry and the children admired and rode the horses along the mountain trails she interviewed the proprietors about their lifestyle—research material for the freelance writing career she cultivated back home.

What a spectacular way to spend a holiday. However this morning it was time to leave. After breakfast, everyone helped to do their bit of packing. Meredith, as mother, surveyed the operation quietly but watchfully. Food was packed or at least the empty picnic basket with its empty containers and utensils. Slowly the children's duffel bags were ready. The jackets and extra footwear were gathered into large black plastic bags. Tooth brushes and hair brushes were used and replaced. Terry declared that his bag was packed. Meredith, too, indicated that hers was nearly finished. All during the process she had a faint but niggling premonition that she had not seen her purse. Ignoring the urge to panic and saying nothing, she continued on course in surveillance of the packing confident that at any minute someone would check another drawer or night stand and declare, "There's your purse, Mom."

Now the car was packed. She ventured, "Has anyone seen my purse?"

No one had. Perhaps I left it in the restaurant at breakfast she thought. Meredith had already left that purse hanging on her chair more than once after meals in the restaurant. Usually an enquiry at the checkout counter revealed that some staff member or guest had turned it in as soon as they left the restaurant. Today they checked the usual spot but the purse was not there. Whatever could she have done with it? Perhaps she left it at the outfitters the evening before when she had conducted the interview. Certain that she had not taken a purse with her for the interview, the entire family retraced their steps and walked across the road together in support. Enquiring at the outfitter's trailer about the missing purse, they again came up empty.

Even though they had turned in their keys, they asked for the key at the office again and once more frisked the motel room from top to bottom. No purse!

Somewhat saddened and dejected, the group got in the car and left. Silently they drove the familiar highway that would take them to Calaway Park near Calgary for a last day of relaxation before they went back to work.

Eighteen miles down the road, Meredith turned to Terry, "That purse has to be there. I have to look once more."

Without comment he turned around and retraced the miles to the resort. Again they asked at the restaurant, the manager this time, and he even checked not only under the counter but the safe for the missing purse. NO luck! Once more they sought the key for the room. Luckily it had not been cleaned yet. Still no purse. Admitting defeat, the family left with spirits somewhat dampened. They picnicked at Jackson Falls in warm sunshine but clouds were lurking.

Two hours later at Calaway Park the day took a definite turn for the worse. First week of August and guests were huddling in their winter jackets. The children took turns at all the rides but they didn't beg for more. They were ready to go home. Meredith knew that she certainly was. Rain had already begun before they left the park. A last night in Calgary no longer held any appeal and the long ride home began. When Terry bucked at the idea of driving all the way, Meredith volunteered. She was too miserable to sleep anyway. Rain accompanied them homeward.

The next day at home Meredith applied for a duplicate driver's license and a new account number at the Credit Union. She worked through the days in a frenzy to get caught up on all the work, weeds, and laundry that awaited her at home. She was vaguely aware that she had lost money in her purse but the annoyance of having to replace all her identification was a much more deterring prospect. Somehow she could not bring herself to start just yet.

However school would be starting soon. She began her round of preparatory appointments. Leaving the dentist's office that morning in the rain, she stopped at the post office for the mail. She had a parcel. Very strange! She hadn't ordered anything. It had a return address for the Easyfair Mountain Resort. Almost racing home, she quickly made lunch before tearing open the package. Inside was her purse. No note, just the purse and inside was exactly $357.83. Although she hadn't known exactly what she had, she did now. For who returns a purse with that amount of money if they had taken the purse to get money. But more astounding was that all her ID was intact.

Meredith immediately telephoned Easyfair Resort enquiring, "Thank you so much for mailing me my lost purse. Is there someone that I can sent a reward or thank you to?"

The reply was a hasty and definite. "No. No one."

Meredith got the hint. She said her million thanks to the resort manager and God and attributed her good luck to nothing short of divine intervention.

DUTCH CONNECTION

Preparations

Rona was nearly packed. She would travel mega lightly. One small suitcase would do until her time in England and Scotland was over. In late August she and Megan would leave for the continent and make their way south using Eurail Passes. For that leg of the journey she had dug Dad's old army packsack out of the basement. It would hold approximately five kilograms of clothes, books, camera, film, and personal supplies.

Dad said little. He watched the preparations in his usual quiet, detached manner from a comfortable distance. Most times the women in the house—there were only women, mom and three sisters—did not include him in their ceaseless conversations but nevertheless he always seemed aware, without listening and perhaps through a process similar to osmosis, of what was transpiring. This evening he seemed unusually pensive and finally removed himself from his rocker and the Western Producer to pad through the house to the high cupboard in the washroom to get down his small box.

Here he kept his war medals, and the shrapnel that he had carried in his tongue for years and which had only dislodged itself after Rona was born three years after World War II was over. His war-time issue false teeth were in there—never worn as they really had never fit. And a handful of curious pictures of people no one in the house knew. We all knew the photos had been taken during the war of which our father did not like to talk. We were careful not to ask too many questions.

Suddenly Dad was standing by Rona, quiet, interested and definite in his request. "I want you to see if you can find this family when you go to Holland."

Rona blinked, "Who are they?"

"I don't know their name but they come from Groningen. I stayed in their house during and after the war during the Allied Occupation."

Rona took the picture. You didn't argue with Dad and seldom did you see him that animated about anything. She turned it over and saw that Groningen 1945 was scribbled on the back. Knowing this was an impossible quest, she nevertheless took the picture and placed it in one of the flaps of the packsack. Later she would sort out how she might trace a nameless family in a remote country of the world. Besides that picture was 26 years old. They may have moved or indeed not survived. How strange that her father, a man Rona only saw as interested in work and survival, could be passionate about this nameless group he hadn't seen in 26 years.

Taken from travelogue:

Train to Amsterdam, Friday, October 22

"We met a nice man on the train who shared his grapes with us—there goes the old international language of food again. He told us all about how the Canadians saved the Dutch in the war and that I should advertise in the Telegraf, the Netherland's largest newspaper, for those people in Groningen. We had quite a comfortable sleep on the train and got to Amsterdam at 9:30 am. We went immediately to American Express for our mail. I then went to the Telegraf Office where some nice friendly Dutch gentleman interviewed me concerning the people in Groningen. It was quite the experience as I had my picture taken, he copied the 26 year old picture and he's going to write up a rather comprehensive story about my quest. The photographer is going North to photograph an event in Northern Netherlands and asked me if I'd like to go with him for the day. I would have loved to but I have to meet Ellen at the Post Office at noon as she went shopping this morning."

Amsterdam, Monday, October 25

"There was a girl in the hostel talking about this really neat restful little town called Murssin where there's a nice hostel. I'm getting kind of fed up again so think I should go there for a rest. Plan to leave tomorrow. When I came in tonight there was note for me on the bulletin board. Apparently the Telegraf had located the family in Groningen. I was to call but decided that tonight is too late so will call at the office tomorrow. I wish I could get the (newspaper) clipping. Have looked in Telegrafs all over but can't find the right one."

Amsterdam-Groningen, Tuesday, October 26

"Slept in until 9 o'clock this morning and packed planning to leave for Murssin. However when I got to the desk I discovered another note telling me to call the news interviewer at home. We arranged to meet at the office this afternoon at 2 o'clock. We cannot stay at this hostel any longer than last night as our 4 days are up so we set off for the Christian Hostel. It was quite difficult to find but looks nice. Checked American Express—only got message and clipping from newsman. Sat in the Dam Square for an hour attempting to write in my journal and finish my letter to Lavonne. However I guess I must not be meant to do that sort of thing as a young girl came along who seemed to want to talk. She was only 16 years old and from Utrecht. She appears to have some sort of family problems as she seemed most interested in my parents and what I thought of them. She was playing hookey from school and had come to Amsterdam by train for the day. I met Ellen at the Student Mensa for lunch so I took this other girl with me also. Man, for a student cafeteria this place has tremendous food—we had potatoes with gravy, an absolute mountain of carrots, a PORK CHOP, and yoghurt pudding for $.75 and it tasted just like home! Afterwards I went to the Post Office to write to Lavonne and at last managed to finish it. Ellen arrived at 2 o'clock and we walked down to the Telegraf Office expecting to be handed the name and address of the family that Dad lived with. Instead we were whisked away to Groningen by a rather impolite young photographer who later turned out to be very nice, very intelligent and well-educated. During our entire 2 ½ hour trip to Groningen through the beautiful flat, green Dutch countryside interlaced with canals we received a running commentary. We learned how the Netherlands (Holland is only one of the eleven Dutch provinces called the Netherlands) rescued the land from the sea. It is a very small country with 30 million inhabitants—that is 3007 persons per square kilometre. Their dyking program is so extensive I just don't know how they can afford it. Much of the Dutch land is actually below sea level and for some miles we drove on land 12 feet below sea level. In other places we could see that the water in the canals was higher than the surrounding land. We drove for 30 kilometres along a dyke with the ocean/salt water on our left and fresh water on our right. The fresh water is where the Zuider Zee used to be but is now called Ysselmeer. This photographer's knowledge of Dutch history just astounded me.

In Groningen we were met by another reporter and stopped to buy flowers at the expense of the Telegaf before I was taken to the home of Mrs. Van Der Tuuk. She was very warm and happy to meet me. Needless to say I was very excited by now and quite overwhelmed by the whole experience.

The original photographer is a boxing teacher and had to be back in Amsterdam at 7 pm to teach boxing so he took some quick pictures of Mrs. Van Der Tuuk and me and left. The Van der Tuuks invited us to stay for a few days but since our baggage is in the hostel we decided to take the train back to Amsterdam and come out again tomorrow. The second reporter had to go to interview another family so he said he would come back and pick us up later and drive us to his home town which was closer to Amsterdam to catch the train so that we could visit longer with the Van Der Tuuks. He even phoned to find out the train schedule. The service of this newspaper is outstanding—they really take the trouble to help. Mr. Van Der Tuuk came in from the farm to visit. An uncle and aunt dropped in with the clipping from the paper in his hand. Roelf(son) and Margriet, Jacob(son) and Rea all came to visit. Supper was very nice—sitting at the table with a family and enjoying a home-cooked meal. We feel loved by this family so my father must have felt very good after the war with them. Eva and Anna still live with their mother. Eva speaks English very well so we really enjoy her company. The reporter came back about 8:30, we had coffee again and then drove quickly to Zwolle to catch the train to Amsterdam at 9:47. Luckily we made it as we have to be in the hostel before 12 pm. We arrived in Amsterdam at 11:10 and half froze to death walking to the hostel. We arrived there at 11:45 and were so cold that we just sat in the cafeteria and treated ourselves to a chocolate bar until midnight. What a happy and exciting day but I am beat!"

I could not help but be overcome by the events of the day.

Wednesday, October 27

"I left a note for the photographer at the Telegraf to tell him(the reporter) I would not be back until Monday to pick up the picture. I bought a paper with our picture in it. Then we went to a store to buy some small gifts for Anna and Eva. Later in the day we left by train from Central Station for Groningen. The trip was lovely through woods with brightly-coloured leaves and fields—bright green and dotted with black and white Holstein cattle everywhere. Some of the cattle have things on their backs that look like sacks. We found out later that this is to keep them warm and therefore increase milk production. We arrived at the station in Groningen at 4:15 pm and waited until 5 pm when Eva came to meet us. We then took a taxi home and had a wonderful warm meal again. We did dishes and then sat around talking. Nela, the eldest daughter, came over later. She's very nice, good-natured, and young for her 33 years but what really floored me was when she said, "Last Saturday, it was your father's birthday? I remember every year." And she was only 7 when he was here. She also remembered the scar on his face and said, "Oh, yes I remember him well. He gave me my first chocolate with nuts in it." The memories of these people really astound me. We sat around drinking coffee and wine and eating cheese until nearly midnight."

Groningen, Friday, October 29, 1971

"Around 10 pm a knock came to the door. It was Isebrandt, the eldest son. He said all he could remember was stealing chocolate from Dad and getting heck for it from his mother. Dad also gave him an army belt but later the Dutch police came and took it from him."

We left Groningen on Sunday, October 31.

. . . .

This meeting began a relationship that continues to this day. Many Van Der Tuuks have been to Canada to visit with their aunt and uncle who actually were living in Saskatoon. My father had met the uncle and aunt in the Netherlands in 1945 although they were not yet married. Later when they had married they immigrated to Saskatoon, the closest city to my parent's Saskatchewan farm. There the uncle had taken employment at the local radio station as a radio technician.

Imagine the overpowering feeling of bewilderment and surprise when my father and he discovered that he had been working for my father's cousin at the radio station for 19 years.

The Dutch Van Der Tuuks also visit with my father and mother and with me, Rona, during their Canadian trips. Mom and Dad have been to the Netherlands once but sadly not while Mrs. Van Der Tuuk, Sr., was still alive.

THE CREDIT CARD

Tom was attempting to withdraw cash from the ATM. Mary wondered whatever was taking him so long. What was that man doing! Although he loved to be independent, Mary knew that she may eventually be called for help. His failing eyesight and the unconventional machines often rendered Tom incapable of managing.

Still Tom did not appear. This really was extraordinary.

Finally Mary, patient soul that she is, could wait no longer. Still Tom did not appreciate having his privacy invaded when he was concentrating on working out a difficult routine. She swayed from one tiny, sized-two walking shoe to the other. She brightened. Tom was slowly making his way out of the bank, but gravely surveying his wallet and searching its many pockets, flaps, and compartments.

His bank card was missing

Retracing their steps to their hotel room in Stratford-on-Avon, Mary extracted every piece of paper and identification from Tom's wallet. The bank card surely was not there even though they were certain they hadn't left it at home. The suitcase contents revealed nothing looking like a credit card either. Where could it be?

However the situation was not without its forgiving moments. They were not short of funds—the trip would be fine.

Tom found all the documentation for emergencies that he needed. Methodically he called the numbers to cancel the lost card.

Still, through drama performances, bus trips to the North of

England and Scotland, visits with relatives and friends, Tom and Mary experienced strange niggling sensations from time to time reminding them that all was really not well. They watched their ample supply of travellers' checks dwindling. Where was that bank card? Hopefully, no one else had enjoyed a wonderful trip at their expense!

Mary decided, just for their peace of mind, she would withdraw some cash from the bank using her credit card. As she explained the situation of her husband's lost card to the teller, she watched the teller's face slowly cloud over.

"I'm sorry, Madame, your card won't work either if he cancelled his!"

Once more they were gently reminded that their funds were dwindling. Tom and Mary reassured each other that really they were not short of cash. Nevertheless they often bought fewer gifts and mementos than they habitually did on a holiday. They could not believe that the card had disappeared. They were certain they left home with it. Why was it not here?

Days led into weeks and soon they were on their way home. The usual mountain of mail met them on their kitchen table. A few hours of concentration was required to weed through it. Mary held up a mysterious envelop the next afternoon. Wondering why they were getting a letter from the gas service station in the neighboring town, she cautiously opened the envelope.

There was the missing bank card. Tom had left it at the station when he paid for the gas as they were leaving for their overseas trip.

'TWAS THE NIGHT BEFORE HIKING

'Twas the night before hiking and all through Stonehaven
All the walkers were dreaming of Dales and of Moors
The boots were lined by the fireplace with care
In hopes they were waterproof in foul weather and fair
The hikers were nestled all snug in their beds
While visions of Herriot danced in their heads
Where he, his eight-year-old son and a friend
Had trodden through rain before reaching the end.

At daybreak I sprang from my bed
Away to the window I flew like a flash
Tore back the curtains and threw up the sash
The mist on the breast of the fresh-falling rain
Gave a ghost-like appearance to objects outside.
NO Matter! Added lunch to full pack and off through the rain
We drove to Aysgarth to meet with the group.
Introductions were brief in the cold and the wet
We're off down the track to the falls
Not much by Canadian standards we thought but said naught
For right then we began to climb through the fields and the rain.
The sights were ethereal veiled in the mist
Little time to gaze—cold, wind-tossed, strive to stay dry.
A short, dry stop at Castle Bolton offered reprieve—
Just three miles into the trek. On, On, On
Battling the west wind, the rain, and the climb.
At mile seven we rested in a shallow gill for lunch
Perched on black garbage bags, heads dripping with rain.
On again—more wind, more rain over bogs on the moor
'Round the summit we finally turned East.
The wind was behind us and driving us on but
Our feet were squelching, our legs were faltering
Just over this hill, no, the next, no, another.
Forever we walked but the rain had lessened.
When what to my wondering eyes should appear
As we stood on a bridge out of lashing west wind

36

But beneath us a rainbow—a full arch of color
A God-given payment for a full day of trekking.
On over the hill to Grinton we dragged
Too early—still locked—the drying room beckoned.
We changed from wet boots, socks, and all clothes.
What luxury—dry clothes and old running shoes!
Kill time in the entrance 'til the warden appears.
A bottle of claret emerges from John's pack.
In celebration of Liz's 60th birthday we drink.
Supper at seven is hearty, wholesome and good.
With darkness at ten we fall into our bunks
Sleep is impossible—the snoring of Joan!
Might well have left earplugs at home.

Breakfast is large, English and strange—baked beans, bacon,
    eggs, and fried bread
A full day's fuel for the hearty and brave.
Our footwear near dry, sun promises to shine
The west wind is calm, Swaledale we'll follow all of today.
A morning of warmth cheers us on through the valley and
    downtown Reeth.
Mounting the hills we dig out the stick
To lean on each step and lessen the wear
On complaining, walk-weary joints.
Our companions are back—west wind, cool, and occasional
    damp.
Sharing the Coast to Coast Walk with Australian sojourners.
Now what to our wondering eyes do we see
But a cairn up high on the bleak, windy moor.
By squinting my eyes I could just see it move
And while we rested for lunch mid an old lead minehead
It moved even more—arms flailing from a distant crest.
Our guide sprang to action
Dashing across river and up over moor
Thigh-high in heather his progress was slow.
Rescued a trench-coat clad figure in white trainers(they say)
A woman investigating the summer cottage watersupply
Mysteriously parted from her partner during task.
John led her to the path from whence we had come

Only then friend-husband peeked over the bank.
On, and up, on, and up
Wind-tattered and higher
to descend in a rush into a hush built centuries ago
to erode away soil and help in the quest for lead
To the depths of Gunnerside Gill—O Lord! Let's call it a day.
But no! Up the other side we laboured clinging to cliffs
Where eagles and deer only should venture
(I'm even too tired to remember—of heights I'm afraid)
Only three miles—I'm told—
We're trailing through rugged, rock-strewn limestone quarries
    and leadmining shaft heads—
Others feigned interest in history—I only plod—I only plod
Mindful that my friend began this trek with more aches than I
(And what again to my tunnelled eye should I see
Another gill to descend and ascend)
I dropped to the back of the pack to give
Solace to my flagging friend and provide her with courage
—She's not last in the string—
I will make it, perhaps on sheer courage,
And be there to lift her should she fall down in trying.
Approaching the Keld hostel we encountered a cyclist
Who told tales of being turned from the full hostel door.
I silently gave thanks for reservations.
Just one step more
Just one step more.
Check in, order supper and into the shower
Collapse on the bunk, until time for our supper.
My body is weak, shivering and depleted—Can I go ON?
Can I go ON?
A hot meal plus glasses and glasses of juice
    and fresh shoes conquer all—
We're off for an evening stroll—just a mile down the road to the
    beck.
Fortified for day 3 with Nevil's extra-strong Ibuprophen
    and a slightly shortened route
We travelled with Keith and Linda
A sprained ankle holding their pace.
Up over the flag-paved climb to Great Shunner Fell

Seven Miles UP, UP, UP over bog and rock
Sunshine brightens the day and burns into our backs
Until at the top we sit down to lunch and feel the sweep of the
    inevitable West Wind
biting through dyke and growing layers of clothing.
Up out of Swaledale and south into Wensleydale
Facing south, the Wind to our side
Down carefully—down into Hawes
A market town with a creamery(cheese factory)
    —we'll go for a scone and some tea before our meal.
Then we're off to the pub for a drink before bed.

Day 4: The morning was grey from the start—and greyer with
    rain.
We walk on the level—this should be clear sailing along the flat
    riverbed.
But two wrinkles not reckoned yet come into play
Wet grass—fresh mown hay dogging wet boots and three acre
    fields with stiles front and back
A hundred or more ere this day will pass
Several small becks to ford and hop on stones
The scenery is lush ever heightened with moisture
My feet drag on through the day
At each break I peel boot and sock from right foot
Press the ball against cool of the wet stone dyke
We pause briefly at Askrigg before the filmed Skelgill House
    of "All Creatures Great and Small"
Trudge on through green pastures filled with Freisen's and
    sheep
We finish our trek in the Aysgarth churchyard
    where sheep graze contentedly amid ancient gravestones
    set at weird angles to the horizon
A few yards more by English measure you know,
We're at the Visitor Centre where we began this adventure
Can I smile for this photo?—burning feet yell "NO",
My heart sighs "yes, of course"
Relieved to be homeward, jubilant to sit in a car
And ecstatic that it's our guide not us who has another six mile
    hike to lead tonight!

But I heard him exclaim ere he drove out of sight.
"Happy hiking to all and to all a good night!"

MY BEST DAY OUT

(reprinted from The Dalesman — May 1999)

Part I

Yes, it's final. After careful thought and comparison with the rest of our trip to Scotland, the Lake District, the Cotswolds, Wales, back to the Canadian prairies last summer, and on to Molokai, Hawaii in December, I've decided without a doubt that "my best day out" was a Sunday sightseeing through the Dales.

We awoke to brilliant sunshine and our hostess packing a picnic basket. The plans had been laid. After dumping the contents of the suitcase picnic basket on the kitchen floor in our preparation haste for stowing it in the car boot, we were quickly packed and ready. Our car wove through the quiet country lanes from Kirkby Malzeard down through Masham sleeping in the Sunday morning sunshine. On we drove along a main road now down to Thirsk. There we treated ourselves to morning coffee and a scone in the upstairs teahouse where, according to the proprietress, James Herriot and his beloved Helen came daily for their morning coffee even when, in the final stages of her life and nearly blind, he had to shepherd her up the stairs. We took a quick and interested look at the unusual array of tasty wares in the downstairs delicatessen. Satisfied that we had paid just attention to the variety of English cakes and meats, we set out to look for the surgery of J.A. Wight alias James Herriot. A few steps from the coffee shop, our host stopped a young fellow—at least young by my standards. He could have been any age between twenty and forty.

"Are you a local bloke?"

"Aye."

"Well could you tell us where we could find James Herriot's house?"

"Who—James Herriot?"

A bewildered shrug and he was off. We stood and gazed about the street. Not ten steps from out feet, snuggled in an ivy-covered wall, rose a red door with the famed sign: J.A. Wight, Veterinary Surgeon. And 'the bloke' hadn't a clue!—giving definite truth to the statement that a poet is seldom sung in his own country and definitely not while he is still alive.

Sadly James Herriot is not still alive. What a thrill it would have been to have met him behind that red door. Nevertheless, it was a thrill to have gazed upon the door and imagined all the cases, confrontations, and shenanigans with Tristan and his irresponsibilities behind that door.

But time had come to press on. The plan had barely begun. On to the tiny town of Kilburn and the famed Mouse Man. Another sleepy little town basking in the Sunday sunshine. Our host fortified himself with the Sunday newspaper in the car park while our hostess, my friend and I, attended the Mouse Man or, at least, the museum where the original Mouse Man began it all. We toured the visitor centre, the factory where one of his grandsons was carrying on the family tradition carving a mouse on an oak chairback. On the outdoor balcony over red-tiled rooftop and past the chimney, we could glimpse the marvellous White Horse made in 1857 by a teacher and his art students. After a quick trip past the warehouse and a purchase, we stopped again and again to photograph the White Horse and the restful green countryside.

Our compliant host refolded the newspaper and piloted us to the foot of the White Horse. In the brilliant Yorkshire sunshine we spilled out of the car to partake of an excellent English picnic of pork pie, cheese and chutney sandwiches, fresh peaches, and coffee. We might have taken a restful hour but the Sunday paper beckoned our host back to carpark while we hiked up to the White Horse.

A splendid walk in alternating sunshine and shade as we

wandered through groves of huge trees and stopped often to admire the dazzling green and gold of the English countryside. All during our lunch and walk we were periodically buzzed by low-flying small planes towing gliders as they began their dips and dives over the scenic dales buoyed up by the air currents rising over the warm earth. Finally at the top we walked along the very crest of what I fancy must be a part of Sutton Bank where James Herriot went often after his rounds to walk his dogs. Then from the right side of the White Horse we waved greetings to our carbound host and started down the steps back to the carpark.

Again, ever ready to transport us, our host was primed to be off along the roads and highways. Past the air training fields at Dishforth where many Canadian airmen trained in WWII and on to the pastoral beauty and grandeur of Fountains Abbey. All four of us slowly strolled the winding paths along the monk-build lake, peered into the tiny Anne Boleyn grotto and marvelled at the immensity of a historic cathedral, living quarters, and learning institution bathed in gorgeous sunshine. We wondered at the architectural genius, the building skill of those who laboured without modern tools to erect such a structure, and the stark beauty in contrast to the rolling green hills clothed in darker green forests. The abbey is steeped in history and still used by local people for church services and concerts. Our North American eyes, hearts, and minds could scarcely comprehend the overwhelming feeling of roots so deep. A long stroll back on the other side of the lake disclosed even more of the abbey that had been under construction at the time when it was plundered and parts of it destroyed.

Still in sunshine, but with lengthening shadows, we made our way home through the winding Yorkshire lanes. A lovely day out!

Part II

Summer 1999! Another wonderful holiday to the Yorkshire Dales with some awe-inspiring experiences. I had thought I might consider our walk in Coverdale as my best day out and truly it was great. However, in the April edition of the Dalesman, Mr. Eric Cropper wrote of an almost identical 'best day out' done just in reverse direction of our walk.

Instead, I write of another great day. A picnic lunch packed and in the boot of the car, we set out through a brilliant Yorkshire countryside for Thirsk. There we went directly to the Herriot Museum arriving early to avoid the reported crowds that have visited ever since its opening in March. The history and exhibits were interesting and informative taking one right into the family and working environment of the Herriot-Wight family.

A short video, family photos and Helen's statement, "You never will write that book, will you?" that finally goaded James, after age 50, to get started, thrilled me.

The thoughtful and careful process of choosing a pen name is explored. How intriguing his writing routine—half an hour spent each evening in front of the telly. I found James' method of marketing his manuscripts to be fascinating as well as the fact that they were not instantly published nor even successful. How close did the world come to being robbed of the enjoyment and healing influence of James Herriot's gentle stories? For those attracted to the instruments of the veterinary trade, there were cupboards and cupboards full of historical tools. For the more modern, there was an opportunity to see yourself on television on set for the filming of the "All Creatures Great and Small" series. Excellent entertainment and a thought-provoking morning.

From there it was a short drive to the carpark at the top of Sutton Bank where our group enjoyed our picnic lunch while watching gliders circle like eagles in the warm updraft of earth-heated air. Round and round they went glinting in the sunshine, dipping in and out of the white, fluffy clouds while we enjoyed the warmth, food, and view of Lake Gormire. In fact the sunken lake looked so inviting that after our lunch we hiked along Sutton Bank for a closer look as it lay basking in the sunlight far below the bank. Our views along the vale of York that noon were absolutely astounding in their spaciousness. Although it was Monday and a working day, with harvest in evidence, all was tranquility and seemingly at peace. Green and gold lay everywhere for mile upon mile.

As the temperature of the day rose we made our way slowly along the highway to Helmsley and Rievaulx Abbey. Eating ice cream, we leaned against a wall pondering the architecture, labor and genius involved in the construction of such a project so many centuries ago.

Winding our way homeward along the backroads, we remarked at the deep green of the forests against the warm golden stubble. Again we passed through Thirsk, Masham, past the golf course, and on the Kirkby Malzeard. Tea was waiting, topped off with an apple and bramble pie and real cream.

Off we drove to Dallowgill in the evening. The golden fields gave way to the green hay meadows, and moors spotted with sheep. The road became increasingly narrower and the stone dykes crowded closer to each other and the pavement. Sheep grazed at the roadedge and rested on the road.

Our welcome at the large farmhouse was cordial and pleasant. A grandchild brought a dripping, newborn lamb into the house to let us "see" what new plaything she had at Grandma's. Even in the midst of gathering hay bales, the entire extended family had time for a quick visit, tea and a biscuit.

Another heart-warming and memorable Yorkshire day made even more special by the folk from the Dales!

Part III

When in the Yorkshire Dales, I seem to enjoy everything. The sheep, the moors, the dales, the dykes—all come together in such a pleasing picture that they paint a pastoral backdrop for a host of activities even if the weather turns cool and overcast. However, no visit is ever complete without at least one memorable walk.

The day began, cool and misty, with a drive over the moors from Kirkby Malzeard to Ramsgill. Some stretches of the road were on top of the world with vast rolling vistas in front to us. The dark overcast mist intensified the green. Other times, we were folded between hills, winding our way down into a dale. Everywhere there were sheep. Some lakes, too. We parked across from the Hotel, donned our hiking gear, met our friends, and struck out across the pastures. Four of us—perfect for three visits with different partners. We strolled, well, a little faster than that—down lanes, across pastures, along paved roadways, passed a viaduct, noting with interest the many barns that had been converted recently into beautiful dwelling places for city folk yearning for the comparable peace of the countryside. From several vantage points along our walk we were able to catch glimpses of Gouthwaite Reservoir, a beautiful and very lake-like holding structure which supplies water to Leeds and Bradford.

About four miles into our hike we crossed the narrow bridge over How Steen Gorge, a breathtaking drop between steep limestone walls into a twisted cavern closeting a small stream. On we laboured up over a pasture to the small town of Middlesmoor. Small, indeed, but sporting at least one Bed and Breakfast, tearoom, and pub. As the tearoom wasn't open yet we tried the pub. Several others had, too, and many more hikers and motorists stopped while we were there. Sitting at an outdoor table to enjoy the view far over the countryside, we shared four different varieties of sandwiches and, of course, a long, cool glass of cider each. From there our group wandered down to the churchyard which harboured a small flock of laying hens and, from the evidence, might have grazed a cow or two at one time. As the organist was practicing inside, we experienced some divine inspiration as we strolled through the historic Wesleyan church admiring the wide-variety of home-stitched patterns on their kneeling cushions. At the door we read with interest the invitation from the congregation for participants to partake in a forthcoming sponsored walk on St. Cuthbert's Way to raise money to repair their organ.

The next leg of the walk followed tamer ground, still through cow pastures and fields but coming out in the tiny hamlet of Lofthouse where inscribed in the well monument in the centre of the square were these words:

"A pint of cold water
three times a day
will surely keep
the doctor away."

Surely no walker could quarrel with this advice.

Onward through Bouthwaite and along the quiet country lane to Ramsgill. Another quick change and we were on our way to a quaint little teahouse in Pateley Bridge for our afternoon pot of tea accompanied by a scone. We enjoyed an interesting peek in the shops before we retraced our scenic drive back through the brilliant green of the dales to Kirkby Malzeard.

But the day was still young! At 6:30 we were off to the Drover's Arms for the infamous treat of the Dales—a Yorkie. The tiny pub served up a massive meal—a fitting crown for a huge Yorkshire day of walking and sightseeing.

DEPARTING MANCHESTER—FIRE/FLOOD

Fire

Susan and Erica left Kelso in mild rainfall. It was early. They had plenty of time to reach Manchester Airport by noon. They had dressed for comfort wearing layers to aid their suitcases in closing for the flight. They were through Hawick in good time well ahead of the Saturday morning market traffic. The rain had cleared. Driving was a breeze.

Reaching Langham at 9 am, there seemed to be more commotion than expected for that hour of the morning. The lanes of traffic were slowing. Erica frowned as she opened the window to the policewoman who flagged her down.

"Sorry, madame, there will just be a short delay. Please pull into that line and follow the traffic into that alley."

Believing this to be a detour, Erica and Susan obediently followed their orders only to realise, too late, that they were now tightly lodged in a narrow, one-way lane and the cars in front of them were going nowhere. Still believing that this was to be a short delay they sat a few minutes. Finally they saw another police woman and told her their plight—they had a flight to catch in Manchester. She suggested that they try to reverse out of the lane and join the lorry route which would bypass the city.

The women stared at each other. She had to be joking. Driving into this winding lane forwards and WITH THE TRAFFIC had been a challenge! This suggestion demanded that they back their rented

48

car through a narrow, winding alley against the oncoming traffic. Not likely! They would just have to wait. Erica was becoming uncomfortable—time was running on even though they probably could still make it but they had wanted to reserve time to refuel the car before returning it to the rental agency and besides she had to go to the bathroom.

Others were leaving their cars and streaming on ahead to the main street. Then they spotted the reason for the delay—hundreds of well-groomed horses and their riders were galloping, clattering madly up the main street cheering on the Langham Callant. The Langham Common Riding!—that annual celebration when the Scottish lads and lassies of the border towns rode out over the common to the English-Scottish border to check if the English armies were looming on the horizon.

Spirits were high among the crowd. Erica and Susan had an air of desperation. The crowd lingered on. Erica, desperate by now for a washroom, ran down one alley and up another street. She spotted a pub in the crush of the crowd up ahead. Surely there would be a bathroom there. She pushed through the crowded doorway. Searching wild-eyed for a sign sporting "Ladies", she surveyed a room brimming with men clutching their pints o' lager and creating a deafening roar. Erica decided that kidney relief was not worth the gauntlet. She sped back up the street fearful that the line-up of cars in the alley would have advanced and that Susan would be sitting panic-stricken in the car that she could not drive holding up the rest of the line-up.

But Erica needn't have worried. No one was going anywhere yet. They sat still longer, mindful of the fact that time was passing. Finally the crowd seemed to be dispersing. People were re-entering their cars. At last some cars began to roll ahead. They were on their way again.

South past Carlisle. A couple of quick seconds for a bathroom break. Some petrol from the station just to see them through and validate their visit to the loo. Now they were approaching the Lake District. The sun was out now. The farther south they sped the warmer the day became. Not a cloud marred the blue sky. Past Lancaster. The time was still holding. Erica was certain that with no more delays she would have Susan delivered to the airport by shortly after noon, almost three hours before departure.

Now they had left the M6 and had only a few short miles to the airport along the M56. Where was that petrol station that they had filled up at two years ago just before returning their car? The few miles melted away and there was the airport. Never mind, for once they would be happy to pay the petrol bill from the car return depot.

Erica quickly parked and set Susan on her way saying "I'll just clear the car through and meet you at the ticket counter. If you see a couple that look about our age searching the Air TransAt line-up you might say 'Hello' and tell them I will be right in. Cheerio."

Erica approached the Hertz Car Rental Kiosk. Good, there wasn't a line-up. The lady attendant was pleasant and suggested to Erica that she use a free parking pass to leave the parkade and nip around the corner and gas up the car herself to save the extra cost of having the car refilled by an attendant. The sun was shining. Erica was up to anything. She gladly retraced her few steps to the car, left the parkade and quickly filled the car. In no time at all she was back in the Hertz Office. Darn! This time there was a couple of customers ahead of her. She was becoming vaguely aware that she was now dressed too warmly for the weather in Manchester. However, she was pleased that Susan was inside calmly getting checked in. They had arrived nearly three hours early. She waited her turn with disciplined patience.

Finally she had deposited the car with just a small extra fee for dropping the car at an airport depot. Never mind! She was through. Dragging her suitcase and that extra package—a pure wool coat given to her by a cousin, Erica was very warm. O well! air-conditioned airport, here I come. Erica entered terminal #1, just across the road from the car rental kiosks, only to be advised that the flight check-in counters were all in terminal #2. However, the air conditioning was pleasant.

Off Erica strode along the horizontal escalators which constituted the causeway between terminal #1 and #2, confident that in just a couple of minutes she would enter terminal #2 and see Susan already checked in and waiting to have a cool drink before she had to go to her gate for departure. Three-fifths of the way between terminals, Erica noted airport maintenance men calmly lounging about on the motionless escalators. Must be lunch time but where were their bacon butties? Strange, she mused! A couple of steps more told the tale—she was confronted by a solidly blocked entrance to the next section of the causeway.

A brightly lit sign announced—"Do not proceed. Fire!"

Erica stared in disbelieve. A few other travelers stood quietly believing this to be some mistake. Everyone registered deathly calm. No smell of smoke whatsoever. Everyone just stood perfectly still expecting the steel door to open any second to let them proceed. There were people with children in a stroller. They registered no concern nor intention to remove the child from danger. None of the workmen moved to explain the danger or the reason for the delay. However, glancing from the windows in the causeway, Erica deduced that they were going nowhere quickly. Stationed directly beneath their section of the causeway was a fire truck. She turned to retrace her steps to the growing queue.

A friendly young man spoke. "We'll just go back to the hotel entrance and take the elevator down to the ground level and walk to terminal #2. I know the way. I work here."

Thankful to be moving again, they set off. Erica was vaguely aware that those behind them were beginning to slowly retrace their steps as well. Thankfully, Erica had taken a luggage cart that had been left in the Hertz office. She was growing much warmer. Outdoors it was positively hot walking between terminals. Entering Terminal #2, helper man disappeared. Erica became aware that now she was mixed in with the arriving passengers. A quick question revealed that, of course, she needed to find an elevator and get to the second floor for the departure desks. She realised that being so warm was not helping her to concentrate on where she was and where she was going.

Arriving at the second floor she scanned the huge room for departures and seeing a sign made for it. The attendant required her ticket. Erica explained that she was really not leaving, just looking to find someone who was. Turning the heavy unwieldy cart in still another direction, Erica wiped the sweat from her forehead. Man, was it humid! She now realised that time must be moving along. She knew she was not late for Susan's departure but she hoped Susan and the couple who were meeting Erica would not be concerned. All these little wrinkles seemed to making a simple little journey take very, very long.

Looking up from her musing as she pushed the luggage car

along, Erica beheld Susan striding wall-eyed through a wide
doorway declaring, "Here are your relatives. How much do I owe
you? I have to run—I'm late. I nearly didn't get a seat on the
plane!"

Erica stared dumbfounded, "What?"

Susan blurted out, "These two will explain. I have to go."

Erica was dumbfounded. It was only 1:30 pm and the plane
would not leave until 3:15. So much for Erica's introduction to her
cousin, four generations removed, and her husband who had
recognised Susan immediately. Apparently Erica and Susan should
have figured into the equation for early airport arrival the fact that
the Commonwealth games were taking place in Manchester that
week.

The whirlwind of events left Erica truly suffering from warmth,
humidity and too many layers of clothing.

The welcoming couple took complete charge of the rest of the
journey driving Erica away from the frenzy of Manchester airport
and its rollercoaster of events through the pleasant sunbathed
countryside for a picnic and on to their home in sun-drenched
Shrewsbury.

Flood

The cousins spent a wonderful week in Shrewsbury and the
Yorkshire Dales. However, rain frequented their activities. Erica
went to the store for milk and glanced at the morning paper on
Tuesday. Headlines warned of floods. Her cousin's mother warned
of floods again and again over the phone. Despite the frequent rain,
the cousins saw little reason for alarm. None of their travels or
sightseeing was hampered except that they might have been more
brilliant in sunshine. A couple of their walks had to be cancelled
and shortened. Rosalie seemed anxious regarding her car and its
inability to function in wet conditions but it never let them down.

The evening previous to departure for the airport, Mother
warned again that they should leave the Dales early. Erica
stubbornly clung to the beauty and hospitality of the Dales for one
more night.

Arising to leave early for the drive to Manchester and the
airport, Rosalie was noticeably worried. Erica cursed her own lack
of co-operation in leaving the dales early and causing undo concern

to her host. Up out of Swaledale they motored over Grinton Moor to Redmire in Wensleydale. The older model Saab coughed a couple of times and hesitated after a good splashing in the deeper puddles. That was high up on the moor. Rain was pelting heavier now and they were just entering the lower terrain. Rosalie gripped the wheel of the Saab.

"Erica," she struggled to sound calm, "We are never going to make it further up Wensleydale to the M6. I'm calling Merv— maybe he can get a train schedule from Northallerton to Manchester and I can get you there."

The Saab coasted to a standstill on the green in front to Cousin James' house. The motor went dead. Rosalie put through the call.

Merv was on the mission in a second, "Right, I'll just call down to the train station and call you back in a minute."

By now, James was beckoning them into the house. Clutching the cell phone and running for all they were worth, Erica and Rosalie still managed to be sopping wet in their 20 metre spurt.

James' wife, Elinor, hurried to the dryer with their coats.

In almost no time, Merv was back on the cellphone. "Train leaves Northallerton at 8:59 and goes directly to Manchester Airport arriving at 12:05."

Rosalie and Erica heaved a sigh of relief. It was 8:05—if all went normally from here, they had enough time. Quickly they were back into the car wearing warm but half-soaked coats. Rosalie uttered a few desperate words of encouragement to the Saab. Pumping the petrol pedal hard, the vehicle shuddered into service. Once again they were off travelling east now instead of the previously planned west to M6.

Down to Leyburn they motored over a highway that was relatively normal except for a few puddles. The Saab was gaining momentum and appearing to be just fine despite her earlier ailments. However, a couple of miles beyond Leyburn, the highway was underwater. Rosalie and the Saab challenged the vast expanse of water. The liquid mass slowed the progress of the car but they had covered more than half the distance when the Saab lost power. Five-eighths of the distance into the water, progress stopped and the Saab, again, died.

Rosalie spotted a farmhouse closeby and waded out through the water and across the road. However hard she knocked, she managed to rouse no one. Returning to the car, she met another young woman who had been coming towards them who was marooned in a much larger and deeper water hole just around the corner. She had been driving a Landrover and was certain that she could travel no further. She turned back.

En route to the water-surrounded Saab, Rosalie noticed two young farmers working valiantly in a pen of muck. Waving them down, she asked for their assistance. They gladly complied, happy for some respite from their wet, non-progressive battle with the muck. They hitched on to the Saab and pulled it through the first puddle, around the bend, and through the second one. Now the test. Would the Saab fire? Rosalie tried her previous ploy. No luck. She waited. Tried again—still no luck. The farmers reckoned that WD40 would do the trick but alas, neither they nor the women had any.

Rosalie instructed Erica to phone the airline. Mindful of the confusion just one week ago, despite that fact that Susan had held a ticket for over three months, she instructed Erica to explain that she was en route but would not be there 3 hours in advance. The airline explained that they could not hold the plane for her. Erica agreed, simply told them that she would be there but not 3 hours before flight time.

Rosalie then phoned a taxi from Bedale. They were almost certain there would be none available or if there were any, the taxis, too, would encounter water barriers between Bedale and the stranded vehicle. However a taxi lady took the call and set out to the rescue. Rosalie also phoned her cousin in Northallerton who might have also come to the rescue except for a doctor's appointment.

Surprisingly quickly the taxi arrived without any water interference but the news she carried with her was not encouraging. Her husband was already in Northallerton en route to the train with a passenger but could not reach the train. The flood barriers were down and no one could move. Still, onward they sped to Northallerton. The time was still ample. They could make it—if the traffic began to move in Northallerton. Continual radio updates. Still no movement. Lady taxidriver also informed them that they had probably bent the rods on the Saab by trying to start it while it was wet. Erica was feeling thoroughly miserable and guilty—what a hassle she had become.

Miraculously, just as they arrived at the outskirts of Northallerton, the radio conveyed the message that the barriers were up. Time was short now though and an upward glance revealed the 8:59 train leaving the station. They had missed the direct train to Manchester Airport by one minute. No matter. Erica, fare grasped in her hand, was gathering up her luggage in a last ditch effort to reach the ticket office and then the platform. She literally ran down the ramp to the ticket office. Asking about the next train to Manchester airport, she was advised to take several trains in order to reach the airport in the shortest possible time.

"Can you write out the series of instructions for me?" Erica asked the ticket master.

"No", he yelled over the rumble of yet another approaching train. "The train is on the track."

Erica shoved the fare through the ticket window and sprinted up another ramp for the platform. A confused Rosalie trailed along behind and quickly pushed Erica into an already waiting train. With a start they realised that Jill, the contacted cousin, had materialised out of nowhere.

Erica waved and mouthed the words through the window, "Am I on the right train for York?"

Jill held up her thumb in support. A couple of waves and the train was rolling.

Erica had little time to ponder the less than satisfying goodbye and end to a wonderful week of reuniting family ties that had been lost since 1884. She and Rosalie shared the same great-great-grandfather. Rosalie's great-grandfather and Erica's were brothers who were separated when Erica's ancestor emigrated to Canada in the late 1800s.

As close as Erica had been able to gather in the haste and blur of hurried foreign accents, she was to travel on this train to York, change to another which should take her to Manchester airport. What sort of miracle should she expect in order to transact all of this and still reach the airport in time for her 3:15 flight.

In no time it was time to gather up her suitcase which was growing increasingly more heavy and awkward. Too much handling for Erica's liking. She disembarked and made for the platform from which she was to take the next train bearing her along the next leg of her journey. The platforms were literally swarming with people milling about, sitting on suitcases, pacing, waiting, and on edge. Everyone seemed to bear a desperate, searchingly serious look. Erica anxiously studied the track in the direction from which her next train would approach. The departure minute came and went. This was strange. British trains were seldom late and they did not wait. They pull in—spew out their disembarking passengers—gobble up the next load, and depart, all in a matter of seconds.

Committing traveller's cardinal sin number #1, Erica left her bags, which were beginning to weigh a ton, with an elderly couple who radiated trustworthiness, and approached a harried attendant. Everyone had the same idea. Attendants rushed back and forth, cell phones and walkie-talkies blurting out curt messages continually. Finally one attendant asked if she could help. In answer to Erica's question about the late train she was told that the train had not left Middlesborough yet due to floods and would take another hour to reach York once it left. The attendant suggested that Erica take the Scarborough to Liverpool train, disembark in Manchester and then take another train to the airport.

Sure why not! In a matter of seconds she collected her luggage, lunged for another platform of the forty-some available in York, and climbed aboard another train travelling westbound. Settled once again she pondered how many more alternate routes and miracles would be necessary to get her to the airport on time.

Glancing to her right at the young fellow sharing the adjoining seat, Erica ventured a few remarks about the flood-filled fields along which they passed. He, too, had missed a train or two that morning but was en route to Manchester where he would be relocating in a few weeks. He was Scottish, likeable and had worked around the world. He was being met by a friend who was telexing him continually from his spot in the Manchester train station. This friendly young man offered to assist Erica to find the correct train to the airport in Manchester before he departed. He didn't say so but seemed to sense that she had experienced nearly enough challenges in transportation for one day. As he was travelling light, friend helped Erica with her luggage as they disembarked. She quickly sought the advice of an attendant who directed her to a platform nearby. However, friend with luggage was conducting an investigation of his own and holding half of Erica's luggage as he did so. With accustomed dismay by now, Erica watched the airport train pull away from the platform. She didn't even panic knowing that another would appear in just a few minutes. Yes, and here was helper trailing her luggage coming to tell her that this was the platform and the train would be along in just a few minutes. She thanked him marvelling at how much help and good luck she had really experienced on this hapless trip. Truly, here was another train approaching bearing the airport destination sign. Lifting her weighty luggage again into the train luggage carrier she was thankful that surely this would be the last train—unless of course, she missed the plane. In which case she and Rosalie had decided that she would take yet another train to Shrewsbury where Merv was waiting nervously at home for a phone call indicating that Erica had reached the airport.

At her elbow this time was a young university student. The two had actually shared the platform briefly waiting for the train. Both had been anxious. Student held the family wealth on her person as she was flying to Spain to purchase, in cash, a time-share. She seemed to find safety in Erica's company. Erica was thankful of someone to share her story of her race against flood and time. In no time they alit at the airport. University student insisted on seeing Erica to her proper airport departure desk even though Erica was certain that once inside terminal #1 she was perfectly fine.

"No, you have had enough upsets today. I have plenty of time. Here is the Air TransAt departure desk."

Erica could not believe her eyes. It was only 1 pm but where were the crowds and line-ups that were so prevalent last week. She progressed immediately to the first attendant. Tremendously relieved to deposit her luggage on the scale and surprised to see that its grinding mass weighed only 21 pounds, she stepped to the desk.

The attendant examined her ticket, did some typing on his computer and remarked, "It is noted on your file that you would be late."

She blinked, "Am I not?"

Flatly, he replied, "No."

Erica gave a smile and thumbs up to her student friend who quickly disappeared to the ticket desks for continental departures.

"Progress by 2:15 to gate 27 for boarding."

Erica had had enough of connections. Although she was beat, she didn't even stop for a refreshing drink. Through security she sailed, no hesitation or line-ups. Thinking that since there was no stream of passengers going her way, everyone must already be at the gate, Erica pushed on. Down the long hallway she sped with only her carry-on. How light she felt. Arriving at Gate 27, Erica was startled to find that she was the only one there. Not even a gate attendant was in evidence. Finally a uniformed lady appeared and took her post behind the glassed-off desk area. Erica just had to know if she had made but yet another mistake.

Knocking on the glass door, she enticed the attendant to open it a sliver. "Is this gate for flight 287?"

"Yes."

"Where is everyone?"

"They will be here soon. You are the first to arrive."

Erica shook her tired head in confusion. Last week this was late enough to nearly miss a flight; this week and after countless delays, Erica was first at the starting gate.

She had left Rosalie so hastily that Erica had both lunches that they had packed for a picnic on their trip down the M6. Alas, two lunches, but no drinks. They were safe in the boot of the Saab somewhere on the side of the flooded road. Surely no one would need water there she thought. But she was desperate for water. She tried to retrace her steps to a confectionery but she seemed to be going against the flow now and it was not an easy passage. Finally, Erica just phoned Merv to indicate that all was well. He assured her that the Saab was running again and Rosalie was with Aunt Marjorie having a lovely, unflooded visit. Erica settled down to a dry picnic.

A flight attendant arrived with several young people who were flying in her care. The teenagers were more that willing to share their water for the entertainment value of Erica's morning. Erica swirled the life-giving liquid in her mouth and throat and marvelled at her good luck in meeting so many saints in her relatively short but extremely hectic approach to Manchester airport.

THE CATS OF ROME

The cats of Rome, the cats of Rome
    curl their tails in ancient ruins.
Along crumbled walls
    run feline halls.

From every crevice
    peeks a whisker;
On every pillar
    naps a tom.

Kittens caper sunlit green
    crouch and peer through trampled blades
Fish with shivering paws
    for twitching tails.

An island of cats
    mid the creak
Of squeaking carts
    and market reek.

Part II
    Then rosy dawn pries
        the locks of night
and Mad Marita
        hunches from dock to door.

A slum of cats turns wary eye
    and rushes the fortress gate
To lap fresh herring guts
    from Marita's salty plate.

59

Part III
    Marits's cane lies silent now.

    The cats of Rome, the cats of Rome
        haunt the city streets.
    Their yellow eyes part the dark
        to raid the herring pits.

    When midnight's flower
        clasps her shutters
    The cats of Rome, the cats of Rome
        curl their tails in ancient ruins.

HAWAIIAN JEWELS

From the darkened depths of the only bedroom of their twenty-ninth floor Waikiki condominium, Mona was screaming. "O, my God. My jewellery. My jewellery."

Knowing that her mother owned no jewellery of any value, Erica impatiently enquired. "What's happened to your jewellery?"

Mona was panicky in her reply. "There's a man after my jewellery."

Again Erica had trouble grasping the seriousness of her mother's situation. "What man? Is he in your bedroom?"

Mona was screaming. "Not yet but he's trying to get in through the patio door. Jim, hurry. My jewellery. Oh, my heavens."

Erica could not fathom the likelihood of such a break-in on the twenty-ninth floor. They had only arrived. It was pre-determined that this time her parents would have the luxury of the bedroom. She and Martin were to occupy the hide-away bed in the living room while her parents were to share the double bed in the only bedroom. Her mother had taken her suitcase into the bedroom to unpack while her father had visited the washroom. Martin, Erica's husband, had opened the living room lanai-door and strolled out for a breath of fresh evening air. The open door would let in the cool Hawaiian breeze before the couples had a refreshing early evening drink and began preparing supper.

With great commotion, Mona roared out of the bedroom clutching whatever valuables she could. Puzzled, Erica walked to the bedroom door. Staring for all she was worth at the dim light beyond the bedroom lanai-door, she could see nothing. Why did her mother insist that there was a man outside fiddling with her door?

Returning to the living room, Erica was in time to see Martin re-entering the room from the lanai. "What are you women yelling about?" Martin wanted to know.

Erica was dumbfounded. "Mom says someone is trying to break into her room. She is sure that the prowler is a jewel thief."

Amusement flickered across Martin's face. He had been accused of many things but never a jewel thief. In his enjoyment of the early evening air he had casually strolled along the lanai that ran the length of the condominium pausing briefly to check the lock on the door to the bedroom lanai.

Shock had rendered Mona giddy. She laughed crazily at her misjudgement but was visibly shaken. She resumed her unpacking. Jim, emerging from the bathroom, had difficulty understanding how three people in the process of familiarizing themselves with holiday accommodation could create such a tempest in a teapot in only a few minutes.

TOM AND MARY II—FOGGED IN AT

VANCOUVER

Tom and Mary were en route to Comox—Christmas again with the grandkids. How fortunate they were! This was their seventeenth flight to the island to visit their daughter, son-in-law and the grandkids. This trip was for Christmas. Anticipation was high even though, more and more the flights took all of Mary's energy, planning and patience. Tom was no longer able to walk easily and relied on a walker and wheelchair. Of course, the flight attendants were great assisting with his movement about the airport and the flights were usually short enough to avoid bathroom visits. Still, negotiating the airport to the check-in took planning and management by Mary.

The flight was due to land in Vancouver airport any minute. From there they took a short connecting flight to Comox where their daughter would be waiting at the airport to assist Mary and ease her never-ending, daily grind of responsibility. How she looked forward to the respite of the next ten days!

"Would those passengers connecting to points on Vancouver Island please report to the West Jet information desk upon disembarking." Mary knew that meant her and hoped that a flight attendant would accompany her with Tom in the wheelchair. She also had the carry-on luggage to attend to.

The disembarking went smoothly with attendants helping Tom and Mary after the other passengers were out of the plane. They even pushed the wheelchair to an open area close to the West Jet booth and Mary gave Tom the carry-on luggage to hold. He was not pleased. Tom always wanted to be right with her helping with the decisions.

Mary turned her back on him and approached the line-up. She waited with other connecting passengers and a few extras joining the flight home to the island for Christmas. But the news was not good. All flights to the island were grounded because of severe fog. They had alternatives—stay in the airport and hope that the fog would lift and they would be able to take the next available flight, take a hotel room at their own cost and come back when the planes were flying, or take the ferry to Nanaimo and have someone pick them up there. Mary struggled to think of what was best and had decided that a taxi would take them to a hotel and there they would wait out the fog.

Just as she was leaving the booth to claim their baggage from the baggage carousel, Angus, a young university student who was going home for Christmas in Comox stepped up.

"M'am, I've decided to take the ferry. I have my parents coming down from Comox to Nanaimo to pick me up and they would drive you to Comox as well."

Mary stared in disbelief. This was a dream and by far the simplest plan of all or so she thought. She quickly collected the baggage while Angus stood with Tom. Tom looked not nearly as trusting as she but he said nothing. Mary arrived back with the baggage. Now Angus endeavoured to help her with Tom, the wheelchair, the walker that had turned up with the baggage, his skis, and his baggage and the rush to get to the ferry transfer bus.

"Have you got the tickets?" Angus asked her.

"What tickets?"

"You have to buy the tickets for the ferry here at the airport."

Mary tore back into the airport looking for the ticket booth. Angus stayed in line with Tom. Mary was vaguely aware that she could not likely have done this alone.

Finally, tickets in hand, she and Angus helped Tom up the steps on the transfer bus. They collapsed on the seats. Relieved to be moving and seated once more, Mary wondered what she had done. Tom had now left the airline wheelchair behind and would have to manoeuvre with the aid of the walker only. She had no idea what lay ahead but they were on their way.

The transfer bus pulled up at the ferry delivery point. Mary saw to her dismay that a lengthy walk lay ahead before they would actually board the ferry. Uphill at that! A gentleman touched her shoulder.

Leaning close to her ear he said. "He'll never make that walk."

Tom's acute hearing picked up the remark not meant for him at all. "But I will. I can do it."

And so the long uphill walk began to the point where walking passengers board the ferry. Inch by inch leaning heavily on his walker, Tom progressed with Mary right behind urging him on and holding him upright with the index finger of her right hand firmly hooked in the beltloop at the back of his trousers. Somehow this pressure lent Tom a degree of strength and stability.

Friend Pessimist frequently whispered in Mary's ear from behind. "Your husband will never make this walk."

Mary refused to think of the consequences. She patiently refused to reply. In front of her, Tom was chronicling his progress. "Not far now. I know I will make it. Just step by step." He puffed.

Slowly, holding up the rest of the lineup behind them, Tom and Mary ascended the long plankway and gained access to the ferry. And Angus never left their side.

Once again relieved to be on their way under the steam of a mode of transportation other than walking, Mary leaned back against her seat. Angus explored the ferry but was often back to check on them. She bought some tea and a light snack. They were beginning to feel refreshed and stronger. The two hours passed quickly.

Meantime their daughter who knew well that planes were not flying to the island wondered what had befallen her parents. "Why are there not phoning to say where they are? They have to be in Vancouver by now. Why, oh, why don't they phone?"

What marvellous relief when Angus, helping them to disembark and descend the plankway at Nanaimo, spotted his parents and their older but larger vehicle which easily held the walker, luggage, skis and Angus, Mary and Tom.

Despite fog, the trip to Comox passed uneventfully. In no time Angus' parents deposited Tom and Mary right at their daughter's house.

GOLDEN WEDDING

Plans

It was agreed. There would be no celebration—just a family meal out. Nettie would get a new dress. Elizabeth and Jim would pick the dining room closer to July 14, the actual date. Of course, Lewis and Jennie would be here from Canada at the time so they would go for the meal as well. Just a small occasion and no cake. This Golden Wedding Celebration would cause no fuss, frustration, or expense. The months flew by.

The Cake

May, at Langholm, was to make the cake. It was to be her treat for the non-occasion. She suggested that she could do the flower arrangements as well. Just a couple of little touches to make the day special for her best friend who had taken her to school on that very first day 66 years ago. She and Elizabeth had it all arranged.

Then a wrinkle appeared. Nettie thought that perhaps she should just have a cake after all—just in case a few friends should turn up unexpectedly on July 14. So the plans changed. Elizabeth made a flying trip by car to Langholm for the cake pans. A second cake was baked at the last minute and cousin Maisie decorated it. Nettie had her cake safely stored in the larder for the few friends who might turn up to celebrate the non-celebrated Golden Wedding.

The day was drawing near. The meal would take place on July

15, the next day, so Jim wouldn't have to work the following day. The Canadian visitors had been lodging with Bill and Nettie for two weeks. Bill's best suit had been to the dry cleaners and Nettie had bought a lovely new blue dress. Jim was being elusive about the location of the dinner but Nettie had a hunch that they would be dining at the Cross Keys in Denholm—a festive and lovely dining room to be sure.

The Pearl Earrings

Bill had planned it for months. To honor his lovely bride of fifty years he would buy her a Golden Wedding gift of pearl earrings. As the day of the non-celebration drew near, Bill and Nettie, Lewis and Jenny, and Elizabeth scoured and searched the jewellery stores of Galashiels. But long and thoroughly as they pursued their mission, it was becoming apparent that there were just no pearl earrings to be had in Galashiels that would be the perfect gift to the perfect wife of fifty years.

"We'll have to have a look in Melrose," Elizabeth suggested. So off they ventured to Melrose.

The women sauntered along the street and into Tommy Smart's World Class Jewellery Shop. Jenny entered the shop, made note of the fine china at the back of the store, left her relatives to the pearl earring quest and hurried to the back.

Nettie frowned to Elizabeth, "That felly over there—Ah cuid swear he's Johnny Ward's double."

"Mom, ye ken he'll no be here. They live clean doon in London noo."

With these words she herded her shopping group hurriedly out of that store declaring that there weren't any earrings there. Outside Elizabeth led her group along the sidewalk, praying that Jenny would get out of the store and catch up to them before Nettie discovered the true identity of the fellow shoppers.

The Guests

Long since, Elizabeth had decided that her parents' Golden Wedding would definitely be a celebration. She had invited a small group of relatives, the Wards from London(Ella, Nettie's cousin, had been the bridesmaid at the wedding), Jenny and Lewis from Canada, and all the aunts and uncles and cousins. Just a small gathering of fifty folk or so.

Lewis and Jenny had made no secret of their visit. As they came from Canada regularly to visit with Bill and Nettie, the timing and occasion of their visit had raised no suspicions. Besides it was their wedding anniversary on July 16. They could celebrate it together.

Johnny and Ella Ward had been biding in Galashiels since Tuesday with friends, awaiting the Friday celebration. Realising that their appearance in Gala might seem suspicious should they meet, the Wards had gone to Melrose for the Wednesday afternoon so as to be away from Galashiels where Ella knew the Mathewsons were coming to shop. In Melrose, indeed, they were and in Tommy Smart's shop that afternoon as well.

Turkeys & Tablecloths

One day until the anniversary. Still no earrings. Bill had an idea—Kelso. Surely in Kelso there would be a perfect pair of pearl earrings. That morning would be an ideal time to drop down and make a final check of the jewellery stores. The foursome strolled over the cobbled streets in careful pursuit of the gems.

Just as they thought their hopes were dashed again, Nettie remembered a tiny shop off a sidestreet where years ago the proprietor had kept exquisite but moderately priced jewellery. Yes, Mr. McKery had earrings. Yes, pearls.

Pleased as punch with their perfect purchase, Nettie, Bill, Lewis and Jenny started homeward. As their road led close to Grahamslaw anyway, it seemed only natural to stop and show Eliz what they had found.

Thursday morning Elizabeth had calculated that thawing the two muccle turkeys that she and Jim's mother would cook Friday morning should be safe. The Jethart ones were miles away. She had just popped a pan of squares into the oven when Lynette flew into the kitchen in a panic.

"Quick, Mom, Granda's car is coming down the road."

Seizing one turkey from the table she ran out of the kitchen, down the hallway and into the bedroom with it.

Eliz offered an exclaimed, "OH, HELP!", grabbed the other and sailed through the front room into the front porch.

Nettie, Bill, Lewis and Jenny filed through the kitchen door exclaiming "We got them—and they're lovely!" Nettie declared that she had always dreamed of owning a pair of pearls just like these. How perfect. By the time the foursome entered the house all was calm but Nettie, careful housekeeper that she was, noticed water on the kitchen floor. When Eliz emerged from the front room her mother was walking about with the floor cloth wiping up water in the kitchen and hallway.

"Where has all this water come from?"

For a tense moment Eliz froze—would Nettie follow the trail all the way along the hallway to the bedroom and the turkey.

Politely she asked her guests to stay for their lunch. They had a hurried lunch of rolls and coffee. Elizabeth hoped that no one would suggest they cut into the fresh pan of squares cooling in the pantry.

"We'll be off to Hazel's this affernin to get oor hair done for Isa's birthday tomorrow." With that they were off home.

Elizabeth was sure she would have the rest of the day to herself. Out came the iron and the huge white tablecloths. She pressed and smoothed. The gleaming cloths were spread, one on top of the other, across the back of her sofa in the front room. Pleased with herself for completing one more of the preparatory tasks, she hummed as she put away the iron and replaced the ironing board in the cupboard. Suddenly Lynette, her sixteen year old daughter, ran breathlessly into the house from the steading where she was exercising her horse.

"Mom, Granny and Granda are here again. The tablecloths."

"Close the door. We'll no let them in the front room."

Meanwhile Elizabeth's stomach felt like erupting from tension.

"We'll have a cup o' tea."

She struggled to relax as she prepared the boiling water and got the shortbread and scones out of the tins. She placed the cups on the kitchen table and prayed that the conversation and activity would distract her guests from advancing further through the house. They sat. They drank. They left. Elizabeth heaved a sigh of relief. She had survived one more hurdle.

Meanwhile in the car on the way home to Jethart, Nettie was miffed.

"Never in my life, has my daughter kept me in her kitchen for tea. And ta think she entertained not only Bill and I there but you Canadian ones as well. I will be speaking with her. I cannot believe it."

That evening Elizabeth, Jim, Lynette drove to Jedburgh to
Nettie's flat to share the cake that wasn't to have been baked. Joe
and Mary came in from Mount Teviot for a cup of claret and some
cake. A fitting tribute to the happy couple!

Melon Boats & Hysterectomies

The morning of July 15 dawned clear and leisurely. There
would be no fuss or frustration. A quick trip to Selkirk for a brief
birthday celebration for Isa's 90th after lunch. Plenty o' time to
dress about 5 pm for their dinner. Jim would pick them up at six.

Meanwhile, the crew at Grahamslaw were flying. Irene and Jim
had come down and spent the previous night for the specific
purpose of helping Eliz and Jim to decorate and set up the hall at
Crailing for the non-celebration. May, at Langholm, and Jim, her
husband, arrived early Friday morning at Crailing to do the flowers
and put the final touches on the cake. The men would decorate
under careful supervision, of course, while the women made the
Melon boats for starters. Everything was on schedule but it was
becoming apparent that they were going to be short of melons. In a
flurry, Irene's Jim was dispatched to Jedburgh to pick up some extra
melons.

Breakfast over, Nettie and Jenny wandered up the town in
Jedburgh for their morning coffee. Almost at the top of the street
they were met by the amazing sight of Irene's Jim dashing from
grocery store to grocery store in a remarkable hurry.

Nettie called, "Hi, Jim. Not often we see you shopping in Jethart
on a Friday morning."

Jim retorted, "Aye, ye're right Nettie. But Ah've been to the
doctor. He's saying I need a hysterecomy."

Jenny and Nettie stared dumbfounded. But not for long.

Nettie chimed in, "Right. Ah'm hoping the operation will set
you right then."

"Ach, Aye, Ah'll be seeing you then. Cheerio," he bustled off
into Tam the Grocers and was gone.

Aunt Isa

The afternoon of July 15 a merry gaggle of relatives met at the
Royal Suncrest Lodge to honor Aunt Isa, Bill's eldest sister, on her

90th birthday. She sat resplendent in her new hairdo and long flowing dress. The afternoon passed quickly with visiting, tea, and reminiscing.

As Cousin Mary and her husband, Ernie, turned to leave the birthday party one of the lodge employees reminded Mary cheerily, "We'll see you at five!"

Indeed, Mary and Ernie were to pick Aunt Isa up and deliver her to the Golden Wedding but fearing that she would spill the secret, the Mathewson's had only told the lodge attendants and not Isa what was up.

Panicking, Mary sounded, "Goodness, ye'll no see me the night. Ah'm going shoppin'" and fled the gathering before anyone could ask more questions, raise Isa's curiosity and Bill and Nettie's suspicions.

Barbequing at the Grahamslaw Caves

Right, Jim was at the door promptly at six. The honored guests were dressed in their best and eager to be off for the special dinner. Setting out along the A68 from Jedburgh Jim continued along the highway failing to make the turn for Denholm. Nettie risked a peek at Jenny.

"We'll not be dining at the Crosskeys. Jim, where are you taking us?"

He confirmed his previous suggestion of a barbeque at the Grahamslaw Caves. Indeed the group was apprehensive about dining in their finery in the midst of a field before the sheer cliffs that bordered the burn. Goodness knows how they would ever gain entrance to the caves near the top of the sheer cliff face. They sighed and rode along willing to go wherever the car might take them.

Sure enough he was turning off up the road for Grahamslaw. Lewis and Bill were resigned to eating wherever as long as they could eat on time. The women were more concerned about whether they had dressed appropriately for the occasion. Through Eckford they went without slackening their pace. He continued to beetle right along the road toward Grahamslaw. The group was silent in their preoccupation and anticipation.

And then they were turning into Crailing Hall. And the parking lot was filled with cars.

"Oh my, oh my!" Bill groaned with tears rushing to his eyes.

Nettie declared that she wouldn't be going in there. Hampered by shock, the whole business of getting into the Golden Wedding took quite a few minutes. Bill and Nettie entered a hall resplendent in decoration, laden with melon boats, and surrounded with friends and relatives.

A not so 'non-celebration' celebration of fifty memorable years!

ON YOUR THIRTY-FIRST ANNIVERSARY

(written as a gift for my parents' thirty-first anniversary)

September 1941

A lone soldier wound his way up the lane to Cessford Mill. Across the valley stood the crumbling monument, Cessford Castle. Rugged emerald fields full of sheep rolled away beyond the neatly-trimmed whin hedges on either side of the road. At the end of the lane stretched the twenty-four farmhouses of Cessford Mill.

Referring to his mother's letter, he saw that so far he had done well.

> **"If you ever get to Scotland on leave, the lady on the next farm says you're to visit her dad at Cessford Mill. It's the farm in the borders with the most acres under cultivation. His house is #18."**

Not even having met this lady from the next Canadian farm, much less her father, the shy Canadian soldier toyed with the idea of turning back.

"But then," he reasoned silently, "the Scots have been more than friendly so far." So on he went.

House#18, with its flower-lined walks and prize-winning hollyhocks, was easy to find. As the Anti-Aircraft Gunner knocked

73

at the door, he realized that now he could not retreat. He was duty-bound to be polite and endure the visit. How he detested meeting new people! Especially in unfamiliar surroundings!

"Well, my boy, make the best of it," he braced himself.

The door swung open and in its place stood a tall, slim Scottish beauty, the afternoon sun glinting off her dark, shiny curls. Could this be a sister of the lady back home? There was no time for researching such perplexities, for the renowned Scottish hospitality had already offered its hand and been accepted. The legendary "cup o' tae" was before him and a biscuit as well.

This is getting interesting. Now I know her name—but still not her connection to the family. The gentleman I have come to visit is a gardener and so is still at work until five o'clock. I've been invited to wait for his return and have afternoon tea with him. I think I will. Besides I like this girl. Silent thoughts teemed through the soldier's mind.

But two more eternal hours stretched ahead until five o'clock. Perhaps I might explore this large farm—all 480 acres of it. What a joke by Canadian standards! Still my own father's farm is only 160 acres but this farm supports twenty-four families. How?

His musings were interrupted as the pretty Scottish lassie was not at all tongue-tied. Her lilting accent amused and intrigued him. Her quick efficiency in handling the household chores as well as contending with the endless round of Saturday afternoon traveling merchants astounded him. The horn of a van continually blared at the bottom of the garden. He watched as she snapped up her housekeeper's purse and darted to the garden gate. Through the sitting room window, the soldier observed Tam, the butcher, and the purchase of the weekend sausages and mince. Hardly was the meat stored in the pantry when the grocer arrived, followed by the baker, the green grocer, and then the fishman. The soldier was no longer content to witness the dealings from indoors. He enjoyed a closer look at the vans, their drivers, and their wares not to mention the banter of the busy, budgetting Scottish wives. Finally when he was sure there could be no more peddlers, the horns sounded but again—the postie, this time.

"What activity these farms enjoyed! A Canadian housewife could not expect that number of callers in a month!" he compared.

Five o'clock had arrived and gardener. He, too, was very tall and friendly. The Scottish love to share their table with guests and the conversation flowed as freely as the tea.   Everyone enjoyed themselves, especially the soldier who unknowingly consumed the **entire** week's ration of butter for the **whole** family upon just two slices of bread.   Not only that—he had calmly stirred the better portion of their weekly sugar ration into his cups of tea.

However, the Scots being a forgiving lot, invited him to visit again on subsequent leaves, and the soldier was determined to do just that. He certainly was fond of that tall, dark girl.

On June 16, 1947, the tall Scottish beauty was greeted at CPR station in Melville, Saskatchewan, by her mother and father whom she had not seen in twenty-two years. She had remained with her grandparents in Scotland while her parents attempted to establish a Canadian homestead in 1926. You know the events: the depression followed by World War II. The years had slipped away and the tiny girl of 1926 was now a grown woman.

On July 16, 1947 she became the mistress of the farm adjacent to that of her parents and the bride of the lone Anti-Aircraft Gunner who wound his way to Cessford Mill—my dad.

CABBAGE ROLLS AT THE RUGBY CLUB

Santa blinked his Christmas light eyes beneath his tartan tam from his post in the bakeshop window. Allison wondered about Christmas in Scotland as she strode up the winding, cobbled street of Jedburgh with Aunt Hazel. The wind gnawed through her ski jacket to her rib cage. It sent the last leaves scurrying from the huge oaks. But for all that—the grass was still green. Not a flake of snow! Allison thought of her Canadian companions she had just left two days earlier in Marabella, Spain. She remembered the mouth-burning spaghetti sauces they had made using just one jalapeno pepper. Might she introduce some spice to the traditional Scottish Christmas dinner?

Right after tea on Christmas Eve, the rolls began. Water steamed waiting to blanch the cabbage. A pot of rice bubbled and steamed beneath its lid. Then midst a tight kitchen brimming with steam, the rolling began.

The men of the crowd kept to the living room awaiting the result of foul kitchen odors, clattering pans and steam.

The next day, the approach of noon increased the doubt. Each of the dinner guests reassessed his courage. He rubbed his ample stomach protectively as he neared the table. The kitchen held smells, promises of the unfamiliar. The opened oven offered no clues. The odor did not increase. The lifted lid steamed and revealed a neat arrangement of gray-green bundles packed in an orangy pool. Allison placed a roll upon each plate and handed it to a diner.   Each pair of eyes expressed the same—regret for permitting himself to this table. Each awaited the other to take the first bite. Allison knew that her taste-test would prove naught. So she, too, waited.

"We cut our rolls like sausages," she offered.

Round the table, everyone was relieved, knowing at least how to begin the attack of a cabbage roll. Still, the hesitancy lurked, daring the tardy adventurers to bite. During the following seconds, forks and knives became clumsy tools.   Adam's apples alternately protruded and receded in oscillating motion. Mouths refused to open. Any array of itches manifest themselves in the most peculiar spots. Throats needed to be cleared and treated to another sip of Christmas cheer.

Finally a right, determined soul managed to wield his balking, cabbage-laden fork to his gaping mouth. The roll lay at his frozen tongue. Great effort forced the tongue and jaws to chew and chew, and finally, to taste.

A transformation from stone to savour! Relaxation spread over his features. It spread and spread around the table until everyone was downing the cylinders of cabbage, rice, and mince.

"Aye, this is right gid food. Gie ees some mare."

Down, down, down, and down. So many cabbage rolls ravenously devoured by so few people!

Rising from the empty table, the guests again rubbed their rounded tummies. Satisfaction plus.

Doog, declaring himself to be 'nay dancer', leaned his stocky frame against the bar to discuss the 'afternin rugger match'. His blunt, square fist held his pint o' laager. Couples 'gay-gordoned' across the hall to the peppy Scottish tunes, stopping briefly beneath sprigs of mistletoe. Friends round the table chatted. Tam asked Julie to the Friday night skittles. Doog interrupted his rugger play-by-play, to frequently replenish the table with musky mules, blue lagoons, and sparkling gingered shandies. Ladies' beverages those! The men had their pints o' laager.

Then it surely happened!

One could not mark the exact moment but it did happen. The

countenances round the table held secrets. Expressions shifted from pleasure to that of very determined tolerance. The odd, adventurous couple danced, hoping that might help. Singly, a couple of the Christmas dinner guests tried to find relief in the water closet. Afterwards, their faces read the same. Eyes bulged, urging the loud, stinking belch. Nothing came. Nothing manifest itself upward or downward.

Each fought his own silent battle of discomfort. Perhaps, by denial, his agony might dissolve.

Finally, the blurt, "The rice—it's swelling."

This was no churning, rebellious bulk fighting the stomach walls. Just a sodden, alcohol-swollen mass contentedly lying there. It refused to digest. It refused to regurgitate. Oh, but the weight! What distended abdomens. And all one could do was wait.

NEWCASTLE-ON-TYNE HOSPITALITY

(en route from London to Jedburgh, Scotland)

at the open door
my nostrils sting ammonia
stale cat pee
burns in the error
I pray the miracle
9 pm bus from Newcastle to Jedburgh
(but those better traveled
tell unsteady information
about British buses)
fitting my hostel sheet
between the stench of bed clothes
I plunge in fully-clothed
wishing a layer of rubber
to insulate
the cat master
arrives soliciting
I translate my undesired
And rigid lie saucer-eyed
awaiting dawn
the 8 am bus to Jedburgh

GETTING MONA HOME

It was to be her last trip. In fact, disenchanted with the lingering effects of five surgeries in last 25 years and the internal lack of haste in recovering from the last two, Mona waffled in indecision. She was certain that at 81 she could not stand the trip. Yet she knew this was the last opportunity to see her 89-year-old aunt — the last left of nine aunts and uncles living in her Scottish homeland.

Her stomach had been worse. The indigestion plagued her mercilessly. She was often dizzy and threw up when she tried to eat. This condition had dogged her for more that 40 years. Sometimes she had existed on water for weeks and still the medical profession declared that they could find nothing. This time in desperation she had requested yet another appointment with a specialist.

"Oh, Sarah. She was great. She gave me a thorough check up and is changing my pills. She thinks I have an ulcer and a benign tumour in my esophagus. I can start taking an antibiotic to treat the ulcer right away. I feel so good that someone finally has taken my symptoms seriously and now we can begin to treat the condition. I guess I'll go to Scotland."

And thus the deed was sealed! They were off on a final adventure of a lifetime.

But even the passport had foretold a trail of indecision. First the pictures had to be taken in the dreadful cold of January. However, they went without a hitch and the package along with original birth certificate was dispatched to Ottawa in a registered letter to the tune of $7 and the passport cost of $85. Mona was outraged. Alas, that was not the end! It came back requesting an original copy of her driver's license. Now Mona could not live one day without her driver's licence so now someone must take her to Saskatoon to the passport office to hand in the documents in person.

Again another winter trip was made—500 kilometres, in all, only to arrive home without even attempting to visit the passport office—this time Mona's granddaughter had stated "Grandma there is no point going to the office. You haven't had your pictures signed by a notary public."

Another trip to the city—this time all was in order and Mona received her passport even though she continued to insist that she would not be going to Scotland.

On September 19, Sarah picked Mona up and they began leg one of their adventure. It was a gorgeous afternoon as they sped through Saskatoon stopping at the Oasis Golf Clubhouse in Perdue for coffee and a pecan tarte. That was an unnecessary addition to their afternoon coffee but was a trip into exotica. The decorative plate and food transported the travelers into a culinary paradise setting the mood for their forthcoming travels.

Sunday was a day of church and rest, and then first thing Monday morning amid brilliant sunshine they were off to Calgary taking a friend who was also flying off on an adventure of her own. Mona and Sarah waved her off after a refreshing lunch and set off on a quest of their own—Spruce Meadows.

By now, the sun had disappeared and the day had cooled but Mona was anticipating the wonder of this facility that she had so often seen on TV. She was certain that it must be immense. Luck was on their side—there was to be no competition today and so the two could drive right onto the grounds and walk to the three meadows where competitions were held. Mona kept thinking the meadows looked much bigger on the screen. In the back corrals, horses and riders were training and, marvellously, there were few people about. What a wonderful way to tour the grounds!

That night was spent with relatives. Sarah had a bracing fall hike in the morning along one of the city creeks and valleys. It was also a welcome respite from Mona's constant worrying out loud and reading road signs that had no bearing on their destination. Sarah wondered about the wisdom of taking Mona on this trip. Could she stand Mona's vocal worrying about things over which she had no control and which Sarah would have to cope with or do for her?

Suddenly lunch was over and it was time to leave for the Park and Jet. Sarah had briefly toyed with the idea of leaving Mona at the airport with the luggage and going to the Park and Jet alone. She instantly knew that that would not wash with Mona. She would never consider being left in Calgary Airport alone for even one second. So even though it was more climbing around and handling luggage, they would go to the Park and Jet together, let the bus boy transfer the luggage and be driven back to the airport.

It worked and Mona seemed to be settling in to the scheme of things.

The flight was fine. Made so because Sarah beetled right over to the straight seats in front of the washrooms and prayed that she wasn't bunking in someone's seat. Three seats to herself! This was great and Mona would not be crowded now, either. In addition the flight was short—whole hour less aided by strong tailwinds, the spinoff of the Caribbean hurricanes.

Picking up the rental car went quickly as well and Mona and Sarah were off around four roundabouts, exiting just one exit too soon. Both agreed that the expanse of water, the castle in the distance and the numerous roundabouts on this stretch of the M8 were not familiar. The sun, when it peeked through, seemed to be in the wrong place, too. But still they followed the road amidst considerable traffic at 8 am as commuters streamed to work. Finally Sarah nearly ran out of M8 and pulled into what she discovered must be a shipyard office in Greenock.

Yes, they were headed for the Irish Sea instead of Edinburgh. They had taken a wrong turn off the final roundabout at the airport. Mona suddenly remembered, too, that her husband had been stationed on a ship in Greenock port for over three months during WWII awaiting orders to sail for Sicily. Sarah's mind reeled—why had Mona not recollected that Greenock was on the West coast of her country 30 miles ago? All the signs had indicated that they were heading for Greenock and Sarah had simply thought the M8 had been rerouted. The map, of course, was in the luggage in the rear seat of the car. However, retracing their previous 30 miles was pleasant enough and they had seen some new country. Why complain except that they would be late to Cousin Mary's for morning coffee!

They did arrive at Mary's house in Walkerburn at 11 am and enjoyed a welcome cup of coffee and bacon butty. Refuelled they soldiered on to Jedburgh, arriving just as the lunch was arriving via another cousin. All was well. Except that Mona was now worrying again—this time about how they would ever get home. Sarah drew in her horns and mentally collapsed, enjoyed the marvellous quiche, and resigned herself to a three-week holiday of coping with an 80-year-old worrier.

The joy of it all was that they would often travel together by daylight but every night they would occupy different beds and even different households. There was a God after all!

BEFRIENDING HYACINTH

There we sat basking in the lap of luxury, partaking of English High Tea in the Hacienda Dining Lounge at the Sunscape Tulum Resort on the Mayan Riviera in Mexico. We were enjoying reprieve from the heat and a sit down for a couple of minutes' entertainment en route to our room to freshen up for dining out before the best entertainment of the week—Mexican Folk Dancing. My husband's countenance faltered. I instinctively knew Hyacinth had arrived even though my back was to the entrance. Then, in she breezed, leopard sunhat flopping slightly, husband Richard lagging at a suitable and respectful distance.

"There you are!" She gasped, beaming a quick smile in our direction and turning immediately to the mere shadow of a man that followed her. "Come along, Richard, let's have some afternoon tea."

We knew we were in for another episode.

Both were trim, and spare, almost gaunt. However, Hyacinth commandeered her entire location—the room she entered, the air from which she drew her breath, and the spaces where she cast her glances, while Richard, although taller, appeared to beg for the floor space upon which he trod and apologise for the air he inhaled. Yet Richard was a doctor, specializing in 'men's problems in bedroom'. However, when my husband's reoccurring sore toe reared its ugly head, we discovered Richard's knowledge of gout was close to non-

84

existent, but then we should have known that 'men's bedroom inefficiency' is seldom related to gout.

And that's how it continued throughout the week. Everywhere we went—gym, beach, evening dining, bikini fashion show, Hyacinth was there. Immaculately dressed, social climbing, and trailing a reluctant Richard to the gym, tennis court, shopping in Playa Del Carmen, beach, the swimming pool. She cut quite a figure.

We even went for dinner with them one evening. True to character, Hyacinth argued with the waiter about the clams in red wine stating that they did not go well together but she ordered it anyway, ate most of it, and then sent it back saying it was not good and she would instead order the shrimp appetiser which the rest of us had ordered first.

Were we imagining it or was our service that evening slightly less than the usual standard? No, it was definitely but politely lacking. Little things—we weren't offered refills in our water glasses, weren't asked what beverages we would like, weren't offered flaming Spanish coffee with its flamboyant preparation demonstration.

Before departing for the frozen North later that week, we chose to dine one last evening at the Hacienda Dining Lounge. We were shocked to see our usual friendly waiter busying himself in the outer reaches of the restaurant. On former evenings he had beetled right over to our table with a wide smile and icy-water jug. Brushing the few remaining crumbs from the immaculate table cloth, and hissing at the resident cat to begone, he had filled our goblets while regaling us with the news of the best nightly specials, the weather, and his family.

Tonight we were fortunate to catch the occasional glimpse of his disappearing stocky back. Finally an inexperienced young waiter attended our table. We politely ordered and settled back in perplexity to ponder the change of attitude. Near the end of our meal, our former waiter, circling the floor with a water jug, paused to refill our empty goblets.

"You are friends with the other couple?"

Speechless, we smiled lamely. Just how does one explain, using international language, one's relationship with Hyacinth?

SUZIE COME HOME

Suzie was nearly twelve years old. In canine years that was well into her eighties. Still, she enjoyed a good supply of energy.

Maura of York, England, had already rung her parents in Malaga, Spain that New Year's morning to share hogmanay greetings. When telephone purred late that afternoon and Maura heard her mother's voice for the second time that day, she immediately sensed that something was amiss.

"Suzie's gone." Sherma blurted. "We were just taking her for an afternoon walk. We were in the back garden when Dad bent down to snap on her leash. Suzie gave a quick start, hurled herself out of his grasp and was gone out through the garden gate. When we got to the lane, she was gone from sight. We are so upset—we have called all our friends but no one has seen her. We just hope that she doesn't get hurt. What a terrible shock."

Maura and Ed ate their evening meal with friends, expecting the phone to ring at any moment explaining Suzie's sudden absence or at least announcing that she was back home. That call didn't arrive that night or the next day or any of the days that followed. Suzie had literally disappeared into thin air. Notes left in the neighborhood grocery store, searches by friends and neighbors, frequent calls and whistles from the doorstep early in the morning and late at night produced not one hair from Suzie's golden coat.

Sherma and Tom persisted. She couldn't have gone far. But as the months went by and absolutely no one in the neighborhood had sighted her, even Sherma began to doubt Suzie's well-being. Finally in October, nine months after Suzie's disappearance, Sherma disposed of Suzie's water bowl, her dish, and her bed. Their empty presence had been torture, boring Suzie's absence and their loneliness into their minds and hearts relentlessly.

The Suzie-less days continued into the shorter days and pre-Christmas season. At nights, before the fireplace, Sherma's knitting needles clicked as Tom read. Bedtime was strange and empty without a dog to walk just before lights out. But slowly the new, dogless routine was becoming just bearable.

Christmas Day was warm. The Jordans were to call about 2 pm to take Sherma and Tom to the Castle Restaurant for their Christmas dinner. The afternoon passed in a round of well-presented dishes, delicacies, sweets and wine. Sensing that darkness would fall quickly, the foursome turned for home in the Jordan's Peugeot. A pleasant contentedness had enveloped the two couples as they sensed their privileged lives. Sherma was overcome with a feeling of comfort that she hadn't enjoyed for months. All felt right—the moon was in its orbit and the heavens were in their place. Did she even feel at ease with Suzie? Suzie? Suzie? She felt her close. How could this be? In her mind's eye, Sherma thought she saw Suzie sitting patiently before their garden gate, backside to the street expectantly awaiting the gate to open and admit her to her home of all these years.

Gently shaking away the dream, Sherma peered from the window in the rear seat of the Peugeot. Turning her head slightly to glimpse the street ahead as they turned the last corner, Sherma gasped. There sat Suzie—in real life. Just as she had imagined—backside to the street waiting for the gate to open and admit her to her own yard. As the car stopped Suzie turned to Sherma and Tom and whirled around their ankles and knees in a merry dance yelping excitedly. Through the opened gate she shot and straight up to the door. Sleek and well-groomed, she waltzed into the hall, straight to the corner of the kitchen which had held her dishes and bed. No doubt, no cursory investigation, just the quiet assuredness of an animal who had been there every day of her life.

What a blessed Christmas! Maura and Ed, back in York, were surely impressed with the magical element of this Christmas phone

call.   What peace and warmth it contributed to the joy of this
season!

EN ROUTE TO IONA AND THE DEVIL'S

CAUSEWAY

Erica and Susan were growing to love their annual jaunts together. This second trip to the British Isles proved to be special from the start. They had been to England to visit various friends, met Erica's new-found distant relatives and had just yesterday arrived in Kelso to find that they were slated to participate in the Kelso Civic Week Parade.

The costumes passed dress rehearsal—Maura's neighbors were so gifted at costume design and were whizzes at sewing a fine seam. Erica and Susan were transformed for the parade into a dragonfly and an orange & black wasp. The Broomlea entry—The Queen Bee's Jubilee in honor of the Queen's Jubilee that year won, of course, even in the rain.

The next morning Erica, Susan and Maura were off to Iona. It was cool to be sure but they thoroughly enjoyed their picnic in the car on the shores of Loch Lomond. Erica drove on in the brilliant emerald countryside. The miles fell away and soon they were in Oban. Here they would stay the night before ferrying to Iona and Staffa with its Devil's Causeway, a peculiar columnar black rock formation said to lead under the Irish Sea all the way from Staffa to Ireland. As soon as they had booked their trips for the next day, and found a B & B they went for a quick walking tour of the seaside town. Maura was quick to suggest that they reserve tickets for McTavish's Kitchen and Highland Show.

They dressed early and enjoyed a stroll down to the wharfside kitchen. The fish and chip supper was delicious and fresh—a perfect setting for the evening's entertainment of Highland dancing, singing, jokes, accordion and bagpipe music. During the show the MC enquired about the origins of the crowd. Erica and Susan were proud to indicate their Canadian background but were astounded at the end of the interrogation to learn that no fewer than 42 countries were represented. What a thrill!

As the evening progressed Erica became aware that she would need to find a washroom soon—sorry as she was that she would need to miss some of the delightful entertainment. She scanned the edges of the room at intervals looking for a WC (water closet) sign. During her panoramic appraisal she found herself looking past one of the neighboring tables occupied by a couple from Sweden. He was tall and bearded while she was fair and, as Erica noticed in her repeated search for the washroom, obviously bra-less. Erica's eyes faltered for a split-second in her quest. Finally Erica ventured to the back of the restaurant where she believed from the amount of activity—there must be a bathroom. Yes! She was right. Mission accomplished she returned to her table feeling very much more comfortable. The show was a revelation. The crowd was enthusiastic and the entertainment, a wonderful taste of Scottish culture. Maura, Susan and Erica basked in relaxation and enjoyment. Would they have just one more drink before they walked up the street to their B & B and turned in for the night?

Suddenly Erica was aware of a lingering presence at her elbow. Looking to her right side away from the entertainment stage, she gazed straight into the eyes of the Swedish man kneeling beside her chair. Craning his neck slightly upward to the exact level of her right ear, he whispered, "Have a wonderful life."

Erica felt a blush creep up her cheeks. She blinked. Her mysterious companion was gone into the street leaving her red and aghast.

Susan and Maura shot questioning glances at Erica, "What did he say?"

Erica sputtered and repeated his admonishment 'to have a good life', while her friends expressed their immense amusement at his interest in Erica's welfare.

PATHS OF HOME

IS IT A LIMPING BRUISE?—CHECK THE FEET

Now I don't possess any of those exotic skills that some people employ while driving, like talking on the phone, reading a novel or even painting their nails—toenails that is—but I do like to drive without shoes. On a recent 500 kilometre trip from my home to my mother's I kicked off my shoes as usual. Not wanting to clutter the foot space adjacent to the gas pedal and brake, I tossed my shoes into the back seat area along with other shoes that I had along on the trip.

Down the road about 300 kilometres I became aware that I would need more gasoline in order to complete the trip. Fishing around in the backseat for shoes I retrieved my original pair and pulled them onto my feet over my trouser socks. At the filling station I quickly locked the car and began to refuel, striving to make quick work of the task as there was a nasty north wind blowing and the snow was floating over the icy ground surface in mesmerising gusts.

Scurrying into the checkout area, I stood in line waiting to pay for my purchase. A friendly nun struck up a casual conversation. Discussing the weather and driving conditions, her eyes wandered to my feet and politely back to meet my eyes. I did wonder if there was a slight flicker of amusement there but decided that I must just be an engaging conversation piece. Finally we paid for our purchases and went our separate ways.

Somewhere down the road about 10 kilometres, I became aware of my shoes and struggled to get them off. What a shock to discover that one shoe was navy and the other black! Not only that, one heel was a good half inch higher than the other.

KANGAROO DEER

beyond the horse corrals
two statuesque does
    measure the dawn—
weaving between them
    through dew-drenched tall grass
two pairs of black-tipped ears
    glide with restful grace

one tiny fawn rockets above the glistening grass
    in stiff-legged moon-bound leap
twin tawny springs leap, bound, fly
    and with a sudden twist pursue the other
racing, chasing in frenzied dance
    across the clearing, through the bush
and back before does twitch a nerve
    bobbing, racing, springing fawns
playing kangaroo

Macklin railway track
August 2005

92

DINING DEERMOUSE

hunkered on her haunches
balanced astride bramble leaf
    left paw bending grass stem
right paw plucking seeds
    while tiny mouth madly nibbles

not even a blackberry picked from inches
    above her head disturbs—
can Winter be looming?

Queen Charlotte City
Queen Charlotte Islands
September 9, 2005
(written at 3 am in the bathroom of
Mike & Dorothy's B & B
on toilet tissue—
much to my roommate's disgust)

GIFT

poised upon a mammoth round bale
    silhouetted against crimson-purple summer sky
the vixen awaits her prey
    before intruding headlights she yawns, stretches
lopes before the glare to investigate
    satisfied   resumes her lofty vigil

Macklin, Saskatchewan
October 9, 2005

CANOLA CARRIERS

tiny mice cheeks packed
puffed with purple black oilseeds
four-legged transports
slave through the winter
across the 300 metre snowyard
until farmworkers checking the wheat bin
pry open the hatch
complete transformation—
'canola spread' covers entire wheat bin

— — — — — — —

farmer pulls on his cowboy boots
empty last evening
by morning—1/3 cup of canola seed
fills the toes

Macklin, Saskatchewan
November 9, 2006

95

CHRISTMAS CHEER

The man and the boy heard it
    as they hefted their axes to cut the firewood
The expectant father heard it
    as he checked the snow-covered picnic table
Her sister heard it from the cabin veranda

—the purling leaping rill
    bubbling through the winter poplars
pushing a creek bed through the frozen snow
    over fallen trunks, around snow-capped stumps

An awesome gift of wonder
    A treat of merriment, laughter and mystery
rippling, chortling
    gushing from the upper muskeg

winter springs spewing a gift of life

Greenwater Lake Park
December 25, 2005

GEESE ON THE BARN

Craning their white-slit necks
in search of open water
they strut their frustration
upon the frost-rhymed shingles
honking their confusion
into the intense fog
shrouding the iced-over lake

Macklin Lake
April 26, 2006

97

HOARFROST, HORSES, AND HAPPINESS

(published in "Western People", February 15, 1979)
Those Saturday mornings were always clear and cold;
Tiny prisms of color shivered the winter air
And clouds rolled past the washroom door
When Daddy set in the pail of fresh water.

When the chores were done and the water trough filled,
The small, sputtering fire in the cutter was built.
Inside the house, the porridge pot refused to clean
Mommy, nuisanced by my help, beat the clock to clean the
    house.
Back and forth I rushed to the frost-painted window
To scratch holes and check the doings outside.

Too excited to eat, I mouthed early dinner
To allow Daddy time to fit out the horses.
He groomed their coats to a gloss as usual,
He braided their tails with coloured wool.
The horses were harnessed with special care,
Scotch tops and bells lent the holiday touch.
Meanwhile inside the house, we washed dishes.
Again I waited and waited for Mommy to dress.
Finally Daddy was ready.
He drove the cutter up close to the house.
The horses puffed breaths of smoke.
Mommy and I crouched through the cutter door and inhaled the
    odour
Of damp, burning firewood, harness and horses.
Each settled squarely to balance the load
While horses tossed their scotch-topped arches.
They fidgeted, jingling,
As Daddy loaded the cream can and egg crate
And Mommy checked to be sure she had the grocery list.

Teams and horse-drawn toboggans were already passing
On the snow-packed trail through the fields.
Our horses tugged at their bits.
My heart was bursting inside my chest;
I could hardly breathe.

Finally the Percheron pair felt the slap of the reins—Giddy up!
They frisked over brittle, crusted snow onto the sleigh trail
Packed down by their hoofs as they hauled manure each day.
A slight turn to the right and we had joined the main track
That led through stubbled and fallowed fields
From farm to farm and then to town.

Daddy's round, strong hands tended the slippery, shiny reins
Reins that pulled and gave in rhythm with dapple-gray
    clip-clop.
And then, he trustingly handed those communicating lines to
    me.
He rolled his cigarette and opened the smoke-stained window
To let out the smoke he said.
He let in the all of outside—
He let in the close, warm smell of the horses.
Tiny bits of snow flew in my face and onto the furnace.
I gained importance with each powerful Percheron stride.

The sharp, shimmering cold amplified the jingle
Of single-tree chains and bell-studded harness.
Horses' hoofs crunched to the creak of stiff cutter runners.
A neigh, a snort split the frost-frozen air.

Then from the top of that mountainous hill,
We sighted the awaited town.
The sunshine-haloed gathering of shops beckoned and called
The team quickened its pace.
When the eggs and cream had been stored in the creamery,
And Mommy and I dropped off on Main Street,
Then Daddy and his proudly strutting team
Threaded their way through the streets to the barn.

At the barn the cutter was parked, not locked,
And the dappled pair unhitched.

Their mouths were relieved of controlling bits.
Their backs were freed from binding straps.
Polly and Dick received their earned rewards—
A drink, some oats, and a rest—
Until with lengthening shadows and grocery-burdened cutter
The homeward trip began.

IN SEARCH OF GREY OWL'S CABIN

July 2005

Monsoons

plans were painstaking   laborious
homemade soup, beer buns
borrowed tents, resurrected
sleeping bags,
purchased sleeping mats,
water, propane tanks, snacks, homemade cookies,
mountains of ziplock bags, oilskin clothes bags, tarps
the list was endless—
finding appropriate clothing for four adults
unaccustomed to camping and paddling
and to boot—
it was January in July temperature-wise

my niece and her newly-acquired husband
would lead the extravaganza—
her middle-aged parents,
my husband and I
(her aunt and uncle),
and our visiting relatives from Scotland
nuptials had led the trip a hundred times—
for scouts, cubs, brownies, and campers
all aged eight and up—nothing to it!
we were primed to be off.
first Ferrah and Simon could not camp at Sandy Beach—
it was full—
no matter we could just as easily camp at Namekis
but then it rained—
torrents before we even arrived.
Ferrah's head ached from the staccato din
of jet-propelled raindrops on the tarp above the tent
supper barbequed steaks eaten in the tent were just fine with
  us—

mosquitoes nipped away even while it rained.
Jim, with intense allergies to mosquito bites,
sat swathed in mosquito nets from head to waist
swimming in OFF
and still scratching.

the six of us pitched dripping tents and went to bed —
(Bonnie and Rod were to arrive next day with rented canoes)
rain pummelled the tarps above our tents.
still at sunup we packed up
while Jim and Simon drove to Waskesiu
to book our campsites along the lake for the next three nights
as Bonnie and Rod appeared at Waskesiu with the canoes
the sun lit up our party.
Ferrah supervised the packing —
filling ziplock bags with our extra clothes and shoes,
we strove to travel light
still there was room for beer

then the drive to the landing —
what began in intense, friendly sunshine dampened
to torrential downpour in scarcely 10 kilometres.
some of us lucky canoers were still in our vehicles;
some at the canoe launch huddled under trees.
finally at three o'clock
canoes loaded to the gunwales
we eased ourselves in
shrouded in rain capes
began an awkward paddle up the creek against swollencurrent.
turning circles
as we strove to get the knack of paddling
with an inexperienced partner,
glowering clouds giving up steady rain
to the accompaniment of millions of buzzing, biting mosquitoes.

after only three hundred yards we gaped at the barrier —
portage already!
heaved canoes up and out of the water onto the waiting jigger.
Simon,

knowing he would have to return with his jigger and the double
jigger alone, ran the legs off Jim(unsuspecting coureur de bois)
over the next kilometer
to the far landing.

Mosquitoes

asthmatic, Eliz knew she would be useless
pushing the canoe-laden jigger,
elected to walk the sodden track,
smothered in rain-cape against the rain
and growing misery of mosquitoes.
on reaching the landing, Jim stood humped against
an aspen trunk, muttering to me accusingly,
"I never put you through this misery in Scotland."
turning my eye to happier moments
we awaited the portagers.
 Ferrah's kidney infection loomed.

Canoes

finally over the portage,
back in the canoes we sought to try harder
to be more efficient canoeists and
make the distance fall away more quickly.
alas performance on the final 200 metres of creek
was much the same.
into the lake we spilled at 4 o'clock
to hold counsel—
according to the campsite booked
we were required to make the far end of the lake by nightfall
in the rain and mosquitoes
and mindful of our progress in the previous hour,
twelve kilomteres loomed impossible.
we chose the unbooked campsite at the creek mouth,
choosing an early night and an early start next day.
food and drinks restored the spirit.
warm clothes held us against the night.
mosquitoes plagued each step.
again the rain poured down.
morning came early.

storming the camp kitchen
shared with a gazillion mosquitoes attracted by warmth
Ferrah brewed the coffee
fried Bacon and Eggs.

my coffee mug and I
sought the solitude of the overturned canoes
along the shoreline.
I weighed the chances of travel joy—
....the mosquito hordes?
....the pelting rain?
....the cold?
....our canoe unworthiness?
too many questions—my responsibility
the decision made—we must retreat—
my husband smiled for the first time in two days at the news!

THE KEYS

Erica and Simone's trip was underway. They were dizzy with anticipation and relief as they left Edmonton behind at 7:30 am that Saturday morning. They had difficulty believing that they were leaving Anthony Henday Drive behind and entering Highway 16 en route to the Queen Charlotte Islands.

Erica had cooked, baked, and prepared for at least two weeks making certain that simple meals and lunches were stored in the deep freeze at home for the coinciding harvest season. Simone's trepidation had come from a different quarter—her boss had recently been on holidays herself and upon her return had dithered as to whether Simone could take her holidays at this time. So even though the ferry passage and berths were booked, there had been every possibility that this trip might remain a dream.

A day in the gentle September sunshine driving forever west through Edson, Hinton, Jasper, McBride, and finally Prince George, the trees were amazingly green for September 3. What scenery—what joy!

A mutual friend had suggested a good motel at which to stay. Arriving early—only 4 o'clock Pacific time, Simone stiffly alit from the truck to make arrangements for the evening's accommodation.

She met the attendant leaving the office, stating, "I will be back in 5 minutes."

Simone, glad to be standing again, wandered about in the pleasant sunshine taking in her new surroundings. Ambling to the corner of the office and looking in the direction in which the attendant had disappeared, she looked and looked again. Striding towards her was most assuredly a visage which she had seen before. The visage, too, stopped in disbelief and then they embraced. Erica stared, too. An acquaintance of both of them—here for a wedding of one of her former students. After exclamations of wonder and registration the visiting lasted fully until the wedding banquet and they met several of the other guests.

That night Erica wondered about fate, about coincidence, and how often unexpected meetings happened to her. She wondered, too, about the near-misses—if the attendant hadn't had to leave the office at that precise moment, the chance meeting would never have taken place. How many near-misses do we experience? How many deer just cross the highway before we arrive? How many cross a split second after we pass? How many Yuri and Lara misses, as in Doctor Zhivago, do we experience? The misses seemed as haunting as the encounters. Who pulls the strings of time for us in this world anyhow?

The next morning they were off early—in intense fog with sunshine struggling to emerge. Soon they were up and away from the obliterating fog and traveling again through wonderful sun-splashed scenery. The highlight that day had to be the fish ladders at Telkwa. Erica stared forever at the huge, determined fish that, having navigated one ladder, rested in the wake of the gate before leaping but again into the fierce current of raging water. Again the travellers arrived early at Prince Rupert.

The following day they spent in a leisurely walking tour of Prince Rupert eating at the famed Waterfront Pub and strolling back to Cow Bay via the abandoned railway tracks which were signposted NO HIKING. Erica and Simone wondered at the assortment of pedestrians they met there—fathers with babies on their bike-carrier seats, a young group that rode their bikes through —perhaps—daycare attendees, young lovers and a senior couple from Montreal waiting for the ferry for Alaska.

That evening at 8 pm they reported for loading on the Prince Rupert to Queen Charlotte Ferry. All was ticketty-poo. They were on—all be it, high up on a carrier ramp. Negotiating the ramp was a squeeze—side mirrors were closed and the attendant continually motioned for Simone to squeeze right. Finally they were parked.

"Please, engage your emergency brake, Ma'am."

Simone stared at Erica in disbelief, "I've never had to do that in this truck before."

Both women looked frantically beneath the dash until they located a small footpedal. Simone stepped on it. Erica reminded her that eventually they would have to disengage it.

"Let's be sure we know how to disengage it before they ask us to in the morning."

Simone grabbed a handle and yanked—hard. The pedal sprang back but in Simone's hand was the brake release handle. With a sick expression she pushed the handle back where it came from. She checked the emergency brake pedal. It had released but now she has to contend with a broken part on her new truck. Already feeling bad, the pair was now faced with the challenge of disembarking from the truck and making their way up on deck. Simone climbed from the truck and Erica began heaving herself to the driver's side from which she must alight since her door was almost jammed against the guard rails.

As she prepared to leave the vehicle she enquired, "Have you got the keys?"

Simone quickly opened her purse, felt inside and stated, "Got the keys. Be sure to lock the passenger door."

With this Simone locked the driver's door. Taking their overnight bags, Erica climbed out and the door fell shut.

Only seconds later, Simone registered a pale look and whispered, "Darn. I locked the keys in the truck again."

"But you didn't." Erica blurted out.

"Yes, I did. This is a tape measure in my purse."

The evening was spent hoping that the ferry attendants would miraculously be able to open the locked door. All attempts failed. In the morning Simone and Erica were told that they would be towed from the ferry upon landing at 6 am. They wondered how— how would a tow truck navigate that narrow ramp backwards— how would it raise the front of the truck in order to tow it with the emergency brake on—how would they ever get back into that truck and drive? Upon arrival at the dock, it became obvious to the tow truck driver that the tow truck could not do any of those manoeuvers.

Seven other vehicles on the ramp behind the imprisoned truck slowly, oh! so carefully, backed down the ramp and disembarked. The little red truck stood alone in the ferry. Only five hours until the ferry was scheduled to leave again for Prince Rupert. The tow truck driver returned to his garage and returned with his break-in kit. One hour later after attempts with every one of his lock-picking tools—all eighty-two of them, he performed the miracle. Really, his patience and skill were Herculean. And Simone and Erica's blood pressure rose and fell with his every sigh, his every new tool.

Finally they placed their bags in the truck and drove from the ferry. No greater could freedom feel if all three had just been released from jail.

Right from the very start Simone and Erica had been partially attracted to visit the Queen Charlottes because relatives and co-workers had recommended it. In fact, one of the nurses that Simone worked with spent part of every holiday on the island visiting a United Church minister friend. Upon embarking on the trip, Simone had promised her friend that she and Erica would at least say "Hello" to said friend. Simone began the trip armed finally with a name for the minister, not just her position.

Upon regaining freedom and access to the "little red truck", Simone and Erica had immediately driven along the beach in the sunshine and mist to the small town immediately north of Queen Charlotte City. After all they needed to relax, eat breakfast and put in some time before their hotel room would be ready. They stopped along the beach to eat and realized that they were already in the area where their connection worked. They plotted out her manse for future reference and returned to Queen Charlotte City for some well-needed sleep and rest.

Simone checked her wallet for the name. When she divulged it, Erica wondered about its familiar ring. She even voiced her opinion concerning its similarity to that of a minister who had served in their hometown, home still to both sets of their parents. Eventually they both dismissed the idea, chalking it up to Erica's overactive imagination and the possibility that with the former coincidence still in her mind, she sought others.

The week passed. Erica silently urged Simone to stop each time they passed the manse but Simone seemed neither keen nor ready to take the plunge. Finally on their last afternoon on the island, after a day spent over on Moresby Island at Sandspit, Simone turned the little red truck to Skidegate and the manse. As they pulled up, a couple from Saskatchewan were just leaving. Simone mentioned that she and Erica were formerly from Saskatchewan as well.

The minister asked, "Where?" and the coincidence was once again sealed. Rev. Sharon had, indeed, spent five years serving in the congregation of their parents.

Once again, who pulled the timing strings for events and incidents in this life! Erica wondered.

JUST WHERE IS THAT LITTLE WHITE

DISHCLOTH?

Mary and her group of seven to nine friends made it a date—
every Wednesday at noon they had Chinese food at the Village
Café. It was a great outing and everyone so looked forward to a
good, balanced meal for a nominal sum. It worked perfectly for all
of them. Even after John and Vi had moved to the next town, they
continued to join the group. Vi had her hair done on Wednesday
morning at her usual hairdressing shop and both came to the
Village Café afterwards for their lunch.

Today was no different. The group visited away as they
awaited their early lunch before the rush. They were in particularly
high spirits today as Susan, Mary's daughter, visiting from Duncan,
was joining them. They passed the brimming dishes around
helping themselves and then sampling the leftovers before cleaning
up their plates.

Mary reached for her purse. She always brought a damp,
white-knitted dishcloth along so that when they had finished the
members of the group could wipe their somewhat sticky and greasy
hands. Opening the purse a small amount she rummaged. With
her failing eyesight she relied on feel more than sight to reveal the
compact package. Locating a tightly wrapped plastic bag near the
bottom of her bag, she withdrew it. Susan's eyes grew round as she
silently pled with her mother to put that bag away. But Mary
didn't. She withdrew the contents from the package and handed a

110

white, limp garment to John. Vi, sitting immediately to John's right, snapped into action, quietly, swiftly removing the danger and narrowly saving John from wiping the corner of his mouth with a spare pair of Mary's panties.

THE TROUBLE WITH THE CAR

The group were taking Ernie's Crown Victoria to their mutual friend, Merle's, funeral in Kindersley. It was a long five-hour drive but the five could fit quite comfortably in the large car with its smooth ride, heavy duty shocks and well-padded seats. Ernie and Bess, Lawrence and Dot, and Effie would be making a day of it.

They left early—7 am. That left them plenty of travel time plus a lengthy lunch break. They enjoyed the early morning sunshine, discussing the new growth in the late May fields, and the green pastures filled with an assortment of domestic cattle and calves, some bison with their young, and even a few elk, llamas, and alpacas. Life for those in their late seventies can often be fraught with the unpleasantries of funerals, illness, and family concerns but it is not without its graces as well. What a beautiful world we inhabit!

The miles were whizzing by. Ernie was a good driver. The company was pleasant. Jokes flew among the occupants of the car. The sun shone.

Effie noticed the slight squeal first. She ignored it, thinking that it may be a stone in the hubcap. It would work itself loose and the irritating, almost subliminal sound would go away. Bess and Dot began a barely noticeable shift of expression.

Finally after suffering miles of squealing, Lawrence ventured, "Ernie, can you have a small stone in your hubcap. The sound is

112

deafening. Let's stop and have a look."

The men piled out onto the roadside to check the hubs. The open door let in the gently soughing of the spring breeze along with the meadowlark's merry trill—a soothing musical interlude. The women kept up a steady chatter inside the car, very relaxed in the blessed quietness that came with the stationary car.

Lawrence and Ernie declared the hubcaps and shocks to be in excellent repair. They were back on the road in no time. However, the squeal was back once again. Just as persistent but even louder. All five were finding their tolerance severely tested. Within the next hour they stopped twice more to check for a faulty fanbelt, a ceased alternator, and doors and windows that were not properly closed. Ernie revved the motor while Lawrence watched it function under an opened hood. All seemed to be in order.

On the road again, accompanied by the almost roaring squeal, the group decided to stop in Saskatoon to eat. Maybe cooling the engine would make it stop squealing. The five braced themselves against the eardrum-cringing squeal for the next 60 miles. Still the car zinged along at top speed with nary a hesitation. It was difficult to believe that a brand-new car of such comfort that ran so smoothly could have a serious defect.

Ernie was bothered. He felt a slight embarrassment that this superior mode of transportation was clouding their day. Trouble with this car belied all reason. Still, who could deny this persistent squealing that had accompanied the last 100 miles. Lawrence, a former mechanic, was just as puzzled but strove to keep a rational head in reasoning out the problem.

Finally they parked on 2nd Avenue. Locking up the car, the fivesome began their short trek down the street to the Commodore Café for lunch.

About thirty feet into the walk, Bess stopped and rubbed her ears. "Am I deaf? Why does that sound still keep ringing in my ears."

All five stopped. They stared at each other in disbelief! Yes, they were now well away from the car and the squealing still persisted. Was the car carrying a live bomb or…

"Ernie, check your hearing aid!" Bess instructed.

There it was. His hearing aid lying inert in Ernie's hand with the tiny red light signaling a battery that was too low to pick up a signal. But just enough power to squeal its dysfunction to all others within hearing distance. The roar of their laughter at that instant could be heard for several city blocks and a more jovial, light-hearted, and giddy group of diners had never entered the Commodore Café en route to a funeral.

THE GEMINI

Rosalie pulled into the Hanna, Alberta restaurant. She was en route to Calgary and her granddaughter's annual Christmas concert. She entered the restaurant and moved numbly along the smorgasbord of desserts and little cakes before selecting one and getting her coffee. It was cold out and this was the first time since her husband's premature death from cancer last month that she had to make this five hour trip alone. Feeling tired, strangely alone and despondent, she sat down at a table.

"Excuse me!" Rosalie looked up into the face of a woman who, for all the world, could have been herself. The curly tousled thick white grey, short hair was the same. So were the cut and style of her clothes. "You looked alone, just as I am. Do you mind if I share your table?"

Rosalie blinked and the stranger said, "Are you as surprised as I am? You look just like me". Rosalie nodded her bewilderment.

"I am Marion Ecklund. I come from Swift Current and I am en route to Airdrie to visit my family. You see, my husband recently died and I am making the trip for the first time alone. I feel a little hesitant about sitting in strange restaurants alone."

Rosalie, never lost for words, blinked her good fortune.

"Well, that makes two of us. Sure…Ugh..Sit down. Glad to have the company." Rosalie touched her hair nervously and wiped away a stray and unexpected tear. "When did your husband die?"

Marion replied, "Just this past October—another cancer victim."

Rosalie began to recount her story exclaiming frequently about their remarkable similarity of circumstances. Before they knew it they were into their second cups of coffee, and time was flying. They both knew this was a situation that could hardly have happened by chance. Their hearts raced and they silently gave thanks for small mercies. The spiritual essence of the occasion did not escape their notice. How could this have happened?

Both husbands had been farmers. Both loved the outdoors. Both had been subjected to a brief but fatal battle with cancer. One family had four grown children, the other three. So the similarities continued.

Rosalie was conscious of the passing time. "I must get going. If the roads turn bad, I may be late and my daughter will worry."

Marion confirmed that she, too, felt a similar pressure but they were both loath to let this magical meeting slip away unnoticed and so quickly.

"Let's exchange Calgary and home addresses. Maybe we can meet in Calgary or Airdrie and continue our association." Marion suggested. Instantly they both knew that she really meant their mutual healing of each other.

Minutes later they climbed into their separate vehicles and followed each other down highway 9 in the direction of Calgary. The road no longer seemed so bleak, endless, or intimidating.

Phone calls are now many between Marion and Rosalie. They continue to discover similar paths that their lives have taken. They meet on occasion in Airdrie to renew their acquaintance, awe, and healing. Could identical twins share a closer destiny?

FOG ON THE BAYOU

Orley would drive. Middle of the night driving did not deter him.

Orley and Marilyn along with their friends, Harold and Suzanne, had just spent a week in Orangeville, Georgia. They were to fly back to Edmonton, Alberta, at 6:15 am Saturday morning. It was decided—why take a hotel in New Orleans at 10 pm only to arise at 3 am to arrive at the airport in time for check in? They would simply drive the 150 miles in the early hours of Saturday morning.

Leaving around midnight was not a problem. Their hotel had let them leave their bags in a storage room. The foursome had a lovely meal and occupied the remainder of their time at a movie until close to midnight. They left Orangeville with contented minds, confident that Orley would get them to New Orleans safely in good time.

The initial few miles whizzed past even though the darkness seemed almost alarming compared to the light bedazzled prairie-driving back home where every yard had several automatic yardlights that blazed through the entire night. They could only guess that they might be driving through swamps where no one lived. Still Orley soldiered on. He was a great driver and the remainder of the troupe talked him through the miles. The road was good, just very black. Just a trifle hard on the eyes, as he stared into the black road in the blacker night.

But now the night was taking on a greyness—not from streaks of light on the horizon but from mist that seemed to be billowing in through the darkness, looming in the distance and then right on top of them. Driving now was an added challenge. Still the co-pilots stared at filmy barrier, willing their vision to pilot Orley and their Ford Explorer along the highway.

Orley's pace slowed, determined not by choice, but by the range of his headlights. He strove not to overdrive his lights. Still time was marching on. Very ironic was this as they had purposely wasted time so that they would not have to spend extra time in the airport. The group became tense. Their intensity increased. Orley drove on keeping up a good chatter despite his doubts about the road, the time, and the visibility.

As the hazy signs for town after city marched by, it was beginning to be apparent that they were soon going to need to find the airport turn-off. In the gloom, reading the signs was becoming nigh on to impossible. Still with Orley driving and three others watching the road, the signs, and the wildlife, they were managing—JUST! It was apparent that signs were the #1 challenge. The fog had become so thick that one could only read signs that were immediately adjacent to the road or immediately above their heads. Counting on the reduced traffic flow of 3 am, the group hoped that when they sighted the sign for the airport they would be able to turn on a dime to actually manoeuvre onto the exit.

Suzanne peered into the cottony night and glimpsed the sign for the airport just as they edged too far past to signal and make the turn. Traffic was slight but there were vehicles about. Orley jammed on the brakes and decided to take a chance that he was the only southbound vehicle on the freeway. He quickly moved to the extreme outside lane and placed the transmission in Reverse. Prayerful that they definitely were the only automobile on the southbound freeway and for certain the only one in the outermost lane, they began retracing their path.

In backseat, Suzanne was suddenly screaming, "There are lights. They are right behind us."

Orley drove his foot to the floor on the brakes. In a sudden effort to change the direction of the path of their vehicle, he rammed the gearshift into Drive, only to stall the Ford Explorer. Mindful that they now had less lights than before and were, therefore, even

less visible to the approaching vehicles, the entire group in one fell
swoop developed a most intense sweat. They were to be killed on a
Louisiana Freeway on the eve of their departure for home. They
tensed for the grinding crash of breaking glass and crumpling steel.
All four pairs of eyes were squeezed tightly shut. Slowly they eased
open. The only sound was of a slowly moving vehicle passing them
by. Some miracle had made them visible to the eye of the other
driver.

Again Orley fired the ignition and eased the Explorer
backwards along the edge of the freeway. This time they did not
encounter another vehicle. At least not in their lane. Finally after
what seemed like a very long time of peering into thick fog, Orley
passed again under the turn-off sign to the New Orleans airport.
Thankfully he again put the Explorer in Drive and edged his way
off the freeway along the approach to the airport.

As Orley returned the vehicle at the rental car drop off, he swore
he could see a glistening pile of razor blades on the vehicle floor.
They had been cast off by the group's sweating bodies in that
moment on the freeway when, in zero visibility, their Explorer died
in the face of an oncoming vehicle.

CIRCLING PATHS

STRINGS OF TIME

May 8, 2006

> "Please accept this cheque as my donation
> to the Macklin Peace Memorial. I donate
> this in memory of my first husband, Flight
> Sergeant J. G. Sieben.
>
> Sincerely, Mary Gartner"

I surveyed the letter. 'Who was this? Could this be the Mary Gartner who lived in Macklin when I first arrived? Whose children I had taught?'

Jim Conly confirmed that it was. "Rudy Hollman has the pictures. He's a nephew. Let me drop off the pictures."

'What pictures? What was he talking about? '

In due time photos appeared on my dryer (the clearing house for all in-going/out-going items at the Kidd house). Pictures of memorial plaques erected in Aldborough, England in 1994 to commemorate the fiftieth anniversary of the plane crash in February 1944. Flight Sergeant J. G. Sieben had been the pilot and was considered a hero by the residents of Aldborough. He and his crew had flown out from Dishforth to test a Lancaster bomber that had been repaired for a mechanical defect. It had rapidly lost altitude shortly after take off, was in danger of crashing into the village and endangering the lives of the villagers. The crew managed to keep the bomber airborne until it was past the village and finally crashed into a hill ¼ mile distant killing the entire crew.

Joe was 21 years old. He had been married in December 1942. He left a widow behind in Macklin, Saskatchewan, Canada; they had been married only 14 months.

In June, 2006 I flew off to visit Joan and Nevil, my walking friends, in Kirkby Malzeard, Yorkshire, England—a town scarcely 12 miles from Aldborough. Knowing that Joan and Nevil, through Joan's father, had numerous and frequent dealings with Canadian soldiers, their graves, and their surviving relatives, I ventured a request that perhaps we could visit Aldborough and continue on to the cemetery in Dishforth where Joan's father was buried.

The trip to Aldborough took no time. The sun came out while we were visiting, illuminating the triangular village green. I posed in the historic stocks before the Old Court House just to the side of the bronze plague that listed the names of the village heroes. The Maypole still stood guard over the brilliant green. The experience was moving—a truly spiritual closeness with the startlingly young crew who 62 years ago had saved a tiny village and its war-torn citizens. Our trio hung about, somehow rooted to the spot which seemed to hold such remarkable significance for all of us.

Joan and I sought some local personality with whom to share the moving occasion. We looked up and down the streets that led to the green. We knocked on the door of the Old Court House. We examined the other houses adjacent to the green. No one was about. What held us there? Was it the sunshine which suddenly seemed strong and warm? Was there a power speaking across the years to our listening ears? Finally able to find no other reason to stay after taking pictures from every angle, we left.

In Boroughbridge, a mile away, we stopped for lunch at the coffee house. Still moved by the power of our experience we blurted out our story to the attending waitress.

She smiled her interest. "I live in the house next to the Old Court House in Aldborough."

Another coincidence—another time when God chose to remain anonymous. How could this happen unplanned? Our trio bowed amazement to this compelling power.

Just Who Does Pull the Strings of Time?

Next stop—Dishforth Cemetery. While in the immediate area we would place flowers on Joan's father's grave. We roamed the cemetery thinking that perhaps, just perhaps—J. G. Sieben was buried here, too. Instead we passed the grave of Grenon, Sr. Ida's brother...another World War II story. The recollection of our shared and separate memories of Sr. Ida flooded back:

> *Three and a half years previously Joan had asked me if on a planned trip to Temple Gardens SPA in Moose Jaw, Saskatchewan, I would visit Sr. Ida.*
>
> *"You see, she came to Dishforth in the 1980's looking for her brother's grave. He had been killed in the war. My Dad and Mom helped her to find the grave and she came back a few times. She stayed with my parents every time she came. My mom always wrote to her and ...now that my mom is gone, I write to her."*
>
> *So that January evening in 2003 off I had trundled the two blocks from our hotel to her condominium in -35 C weather thinking—'any friend of Joan's cannot be bad.' Sr. Ida and I had a delightful visit talking for an hour as if we had known each other all our lives. What a remarkable find!*

But Joan had lost Sr. Ida's address. Joan's 2005 Christmas letter came back in March 2006. What was she to do?

I heard the story and thought maybe...just maybe.

Approaching Sr. Donata at St. Anthony's convent in Macklin in early May, I enquired, "Do you know a Sr. Ida who was previously in Moose Jaw? Do you think you could find her?"

"No, I don't know her but I'll try." Sr. Donata promised.

In a week, Sr. Donata had the new address. I relayed it over the telephone to Joan in England; the following Sunday afternoon. Although doubtful that a new letter would find Sr. Ida alive, well, or able to reply, Joan quickly sent off another letter the following day.

Arriving in Kirkby Malzeard on June 17, I was greeted by a

near-explosion from Joan, "I've heard from her, Sr. Ida. She's written to us. She moved to Regina and thought she had sent us a change of address. Perhaps she did but we never received it. But, O! How wonderful to hear from her again."

How small is a world where friends on two continents, without the help of e-mail, but instead the help of empowered friends can make the right connections! What magic we weave! What joy we create!

Or does God's anonymous hand pull the strings of time?

ISBN 142513621-4